*Southern Living*

# Bathrooms
# Planning & Remodeling

**A combination of tiles** inset into 12- by 12-inch limestone
creates a rug pattern on the floor of this master bath.
The spa bath, framed by pilasters and a transom, displays
the same design on the raised surround.

Oxmoor
House®

D1528955

**A natural palette** inspired the rich colors of this bathroom. The sculptural ceramic tiles and the glazed stoneware lavatory were handcrafted.

Book Editor
**Scott Atkinson**

Coordinating Editor
**Suzanne Normand Eyre**

Design
**Joe di Chiarro**

Illustrations
**Bill Oetinger**

Photo Stylist
**JoAnn Masaoka Van Atta**

Consulting Editor
**Jane Horn**

Editorial Coordinator
**Vicki Weathers**

Cover
**Design by Vasken Guiragossian and James Boone. Photography by Jean Allsopp. Interior Design by David Gadlage.**

Our appreciation to the staff of *Southern Living* magazine for their contributions to this book.

## Photography

**Jean Allsopp:** 1, 10, 29, 32 top, 35 bottom; **Brian Vanden Brink:** 19 bottom, 23 bottom, 26 top left; **Jared Chandler:** 20 top; **Stephen Cridland:** 16 bottom, 27 top; **Cheryl Dalton:** 35 top; **Jay Graham:** 31 bottom; **Mick Hales:** 32 bottom; **Philip Harvey:** 6, 7 top, 8 top left and bottom left, 12 top, 13, 14, 16 top, 18, 19 top left and top right, 22, 23 top left and top right, 24 bottom, 25, 27 bottom, 28 bottom, 31 top, 33, 34, 46, 48, 51, 64; **David Duncan Livingston:** 20 bottom, 49; **Sylvia Martin:** 2, 5, 7 bottom right, 9 top, 15 bottom, 24 top, 26 bottom, 28 top; **Emily Minton:** 11; **Kenneth Rice:** 8 top right; **Meg McKinney Simle:** 12 bottom, 15 top, 17 top, 21, 30, 37; **Tom Wyatt:** 9 bottom, 17 bottom.

*Southern Living® Bathrooms: Planning & Remodeling* was adapted from a book by the same title published by Sunset Books.

First printing January 1999

ISBN 0-376-09055-3

Library of Congress Catalog Card Number: 98-87005

Printed in the United States.

# Time to update your bathroom?

At first glance, a bathroom may seem relatively uncomplicated—a sink, a toilet, and a tub or shower within four walls. But as a look through the pages of this book will prove, there's a lot more to a bathroom than just the basics. Double sinks, whirlpool tubs, stunning tiled surfaces, rich cabinetry—all contribute to turning today's bathrooms into design statements all their own. Now you can achieve the same results.

This new edition offers a wealth of information to guide you, from design ideas for successful floor plans to actual construction techniques. A special section compares the various products on the market today so you can shop wisely for cabinetry, surfacing materials, and fixtures. Whether you're doing the work yourself or hiring professionals for some or all of it, this complete course on bathroom design and construction will provide the help you need.

Special thanks go to Fran Feldman for carefully editing the manuscript. We also wish to thank The Bath & Beyond; Roger Chetrit of Tile Visions; Dillon Tile Supply, Inc.; Menlo Park Hardware Co.; and Plumbing n' Things.

# Contents

## Special Features

# DESIGN IDEAS

## Layouts ■ Materials ■ Lighting ■ Storage

**E**veryone knows a picture is worth a thousand words. That's why this chapter is packed with full-color photos showing bathroom design ideas that you can apply to your own situation, whether you're remodeling an existing bathroom or starting from scratch.

The first section, "Basic layouts" (pages 6–11), presents a variety of floor plans. Even though you may not have a choice of floor plan, study the photos in this section carefully—you're likely to find details that apply to your bathroom. A related section, "Water works" (pages 12–17), deals with the major plumbing fixtures—sinks, tubs, and showers—around which modern bath design revolves.

"On the surface" (pages 18–23) shows good ways to use surfacing materials ranging from faux painting to stone. "Bright ideas" (pages 24–29) explores natural and artificial lighting, almost always subject to improvement when you're remodeling and an important concern if you're designing a new bath. "Storage solutions" (pages 30–35) concludes the chapter.

**The placement of the window** along this bathroom's front wall determined where the fixtures would go. The tub sits lengthwise under the framed opening and serves as a buffer between his-and-hers vanities. Beaded-board panels and marble trim around the tub reflect the home's traditional architecture. The recycled heart-pine flooring is protected with a waterborne urethane finish.

DESIGNER: DEBRA GUTIERREZ

**Barrier-free shower design** is both beautiful and practical. Incorporated into a stylish marble design is an adjustable hand-held shower head, a grab bar, and a comfortable bench.

**A painted cabinet,** found at an antiques store, provides an elegant base for a powder room vanity. Its depth—only 16 inches—was too shallow for a standard vanity sink, but a smaller (14- by 18-inch) hammered copper basin just fit.

# ■ Basic layouts

ARCHITECT: DAVID WILLIAMS
DESIGNER: RICK SAMBOL / DESIGN CONSULTANTS

DECORATIVE PAINTING: THE BEARDSLEY COMPANY

**Powder rooms** occasion bold designs that may not be "practical" for day-to-day bathrooms. In an antique vein, room shown above features a formal parquet floor and a wall-hung sink on shiny chrome legs; painted flowers dominate. Limited understair space shown in photo at left gains weight from textured wallpaper and jet black accents.

DESIGNER: LOU ANN BAUER / BAUER INTERIOR DESIGN

**Small washroom** combines white wood wainscoting with colorful walls and a hand-painted mirror. Sink fittings atop pedestal sink are actually outdoor faucets.

ARCHITECT: ROBERT HAMMOND

**The owners of this compact** master bath chose details over dimensions. The most prominent feature is an elongated lavatory supported by two columnar legs. Beaded-board wainscot lines the walls, and hardwood floors create a sense of continuity with the rest of the house. A tall, narrow wooden cabinet and a built-in window seat provide attractive alternatives to under-the-sink storage and a linen closet.

DESIGNER: RUTH SOFORENKO ASSOCIATES

**Tiny white bath** has requisite amenities, thanks to careful planning and reliable built-ins. Vanity, sink, tub, and toilet come together in a tight intersection; curves avoid protruding corners.

# ■ Basic layouts

DESIGNER: CATHY NASON ASID INTERIOR DESIGN

ARCHITECT: CHARLES MOORE

RESIDENTIAL DESIGNERS: RICK SPITZMILLER AND ROBERT
NORRIS, SPITZMILLER & NORRIS, INC. DESIGNER: MARCIA LYLE

**Successful master suite** links multiple
elements in an efficient, private retreat. Suite
shown above features a stepped glass-block
divider that maintains link between bed
and bath. Black acrylic tub is on bedroom
side of divider; walk-in shower is tucked into
a corner. In photo at left, a large master bath
next to the bedroom also functions as a
dressing area. Two generous closets flank a
custom vanity that houses side-by-side sinks
and ample storage. In photo opposite, this
new bathroom was inserted within an
existing half-story space tucked along the
back of the house. The room's linear configuration, approximately 8 by 16 feet,
provided space for a large tiled shower at
one end. The wall opposite the windows
accommodates a vanity with double sinks.
A built-in storage niche is convenient to both
shower and vanity.

# Water works

**Modern pedestal sink** lends its smooth lines to a clean white, symmetrical wall. Mirror anchors design; glass shelf provides trim storage for sink-side accessories. Stylish twin wall sconces shed task light from both directions.

**The center section** of this bathroom cabinet, which holds the sink, is raised to a comfortable height for standing. The counter to the left—used as a vanity—is stepped down to desk height, as is the counter to the right.

**Crystal sink bowl** sits atop a transparent shelf in a small powder room. Drain fittings run through transparent glass countertop, providing a design statement of their own.

# ■ Water works

DESIGNER: GERALD N. JACOBS / JACOBS DESIGN

**A holdover from the past,** stout free-standing tub highlights a brand-new bathroom. Reconditioned with a chrome spout and handles, tub is ready for many more relaxing soaks.

ARCHITECT: LOU KIMBALL, STEINBOMER & ASSOCIATES

**This footed tub** affords a dramatic view to a canyon and the hills beyond (hidden shades can be pulled down for privacy). The tiled divider walls are only 3½ feet tall to visually expand the small room. Despite their low height, they are still large enough to contain handy storage niches on multiple sides.

**A deep bathtub** separates his-and-hers vanities, but similar cabinetry for all three units ensures a smooth visual transition. Adding dramatic contrast to the crisp white scheme is ceramic tile trim in a bold malachite green.

**The 42-by-72-inch whirlpool** tub is angled between two windows, taking advantage of the views and the private location. To give the ambience of a luxury spa, the floor and tub surround are marble, and cabinetwork is painted white with solid-brass pulls. The walls are mirrored for openness and easy maintenance.

# ■ **Water works**

ARCHITECT: DAVID WILLIAMS
DESIGNER: RICK SAMBOL / DESIGN CONSULTANTS

**Seamless glass steam shower** holds down end of a tub platform housing an oval-shaped whirlpool tub. Second-story picture window offers tub-side views; diamond-shaped shower window combines view with privacy.

**Walk-in shower** has a striking curved shape that's echoed in floor tiles. Glass blocks bring in light while maintaining privacy; downlights provide auxiliary light.

**This cheerful bathroom** is designed for a young girl. The combination tub and shower is low enough for small fry to easily scale, and the sink features an attractive faucet set that is comfortable for little hands to operate.

DESIGNER: ELLEN ALVAREZ / DESIGN CABINET SHOWROOMS

**Tucked into a corner** of a small bath, sleek European shower unit displays an adjustable shower head and massage unit along with a fold-down seat. Curved sliding doors can be removed for cleaning.

# On the surface

**Pink wallpaper** lends country cheer to walls surrounding a whirlpool tub. Light porcelain tiles facing platform front, tub deck, and backsplash contrast with the dark-stained oak floor.

DESIGNER: CHARLOTTE BOYLE INTERIORS
ARCHITECT: J. ALLEN SAYLES

DESIGNER: MONA BRANAGH / PACIFIC BAY INTERIORS

**Two variations** on the pedestal theme: angular adult bath (shown above, at left) gains its fresh effect from a white tile floor and wainscoting punctuated by dark trim tiles and chrome accents. Child's bath (shown above, at right) combines a traditional fluted sink on a glazed-tile pedestal with wallpaper and matching cabinet accents.

DESIGN: CLASSIC POST & BEAM

**Nothing says country comfort** like wood—in this case, pine tongue-and-groove paneling, timbers, and window trim. Light tile surrounds tub area, heading off moisture damage and allowing for easy cleaning.

# ◼ On the surface

DESIGNER: JOSH CHANDLER

DESIGNER: DAVID LIVINGSTON INTERIORS

**Bathrooms offer a blank canvas** for varied creative expression. In photo above, wall sculpture is joined by an eclectic mix that includes a stainless steel countertop and integral sink, a red tub, textured walls, and wood rafters and ceiling.

In a softer style, room at left combines a vanity with amazingly varied slate floor and walls. Sink holes cut in bowl and cabinet accommodate plumbing.

**Carefully chosen finishes** add warmth and luxury to a rustic, yet elegant bath. The floor is gray-green Vermont slate—in 12-inch tiles laid on the diagonal. Behind the tub, a backsplash made of 12-inch French limestone tiles forms a harlequin pattern. The cedar beams were custom-painted to achieve a crackled look.

# ■ On the surface

**Textured porcelain tiles** marked by subtle variations wrap an oval tub in soft color. Deck-mounted tub fittings are in a matching muted finish; seamless shower recedes from view and doesn't interrupt sense of space and quiet.

ARCHITECT: MORIMOTO ARCHITECTS

**Bold or subtle,** flooring makes a supporting statement in bathrooms. Black and white tile mosaic flooring (above left) lends energy to a quiet bath design; tiles are toasty to the touch, thanks to radiant heating pipes below. In photo above, soft-toned field tiles and matching grout are punctuated by colorful glazed diamond inserts.

**Hardwood wainscoting** and chair rail, softened with a white pickling wash, lead the way to a simple European-style pedestal sink. Tile floor and built-in bureau amplify the mood.

# Bright ideas

DESIGNER: GAY FLY

**Adding light and design punch** while maintaining privacy, glass block is ideal for bathroom installation. The tailored glass block in the bath above is in keeping with the spa feel of the room. Single strip of block in photo at left brings a flash of light to a child's tub/shower.

DESIGNER: JIM WALLEN / ACORN KITCHENS & BATHS

DESIGNER: RICK SAMBOL / DESIGN CONSULTANTS

**Block walls and an opening skylight** team up to provide diffuse light and ventilation in a master bath. Block wraps behind both tub and nearby steam shower; mirrors blur boundaries and amplify brightness. Steam shower offers a glimpse of outside through clear blocks up high and in corner.

# ■ Bright ideas

ARCHITECT: JOHN MORRIS

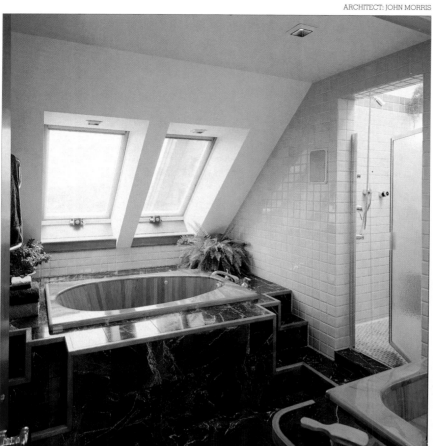

**No room in the house** requires privacy more than a bath. At left, twin roof windows furnish a sunny, private view from an upstairs bath and provide great ventilation, too. Dark green tropical shutters, shown below, left, conceal the 7-foot window that sits above the tub, yet still allow filtered sunlight into the room.

ARCHITECT: CHICK GRANT

**Second-story privacy** offered an opportunity to open master bath to garden: French doors, matching overhead transoms, tub-side double-hung windows, and a skylight do the trick. Indirect soffit fixtures provide quiet light for a nighttime soak.

ARCHITECT: JERRY L. WARD

**Whirlpool tub** in a bathroom bay appears to float into surrounding woodland. Decorative windowpanes focus attention on trees and screen bathers from outside view.

DESIGN: DIANE STEVENSON DESIGN
WINDOWS: ALAN MASAOKA ARCHITECTURAL GLASS

## ■ Bright ideas

**Natural light** from a trio of windows brightens this cozy tub niche. Striped wallpaper and fabric join as a pretty backdrop for the whirlpool tub.

**Light permeates** this bright bath. Sources are all visible in mirror: large ridgeline skylights, glass blocks to help spread light, frosted glass doors, and twin wall sconces to provide plenty of task light around stylish pedestal sink.

ARCHITECT: REMICK ASSOCIATES

**With mirrors on three sides,** this well-lit vanity area seems extra brilliant. Recessed downlights in the soffit supply general illumination, supplemented by a pair of decorative wall sconces and a small table lamp.

# Storage solutions

**Hiding behind an expansive** vanity mirror is a roomy storage cabinet deep enough
to hold hand towels as well as the usual toiletries. The cabinet seems to disappear
when its mirrored door is closed.

DESIGNER: RICK SAMBOL / DESIGN CONSULTANTS AND LYNNE SHILLING

**Stylish European cabinetry** built into angle between shower and toilet compartments offers floor-to-ceiling storage and display space on recessed glass shelves. Pinpoint accent lighting comes from low-voltage MR-16 downlights with slot apertures.

DESIGN: LAMPERTI ASSOCIATES

**Red mahogany cabinets** organize every inch of this formal bath done in "club room" style. Base cabinets, lipped shelves, mirror and tub arches, and tub pedestal all match; elegant millwork ties loose ends together.

# ■ Storage solutions

RESIDENTIAL DESIGNERS: RICK SPITZMILLER AND ROBERT NORRIS, SPITZMILLER & NORRIS, INC.

**Built-ins create visual interest** along this bathroom's blank wall. A custom bookcase modeled on an antique French chest provides linen storage, a spot for the television, and a mini library.

**This sleek wood vanity** and the mirror above it seem to float in front of the window. True to its 1930s Art Deco spirit, the bath is finished in stainless steel and glass block.

ARCHITECT: BOBBY MCALPINE

ARCHITECT: J. ALLEN SAYLES

**Dressing area** forms a transition zone between bedroom and bath; owners wanted a master suite feel but didn't have space for a separate dressing room. Maple cabinets house plenty of drawers, pegs, cubbyholes, and adjustable shelves; lowered counter section becomes a makeup table.

DESIGNER: MONA BRANAGH / PACIFIC BAY INTERIORS

**Antique dresser** takes on new life as a bathroom vanity in this traditional setting. Holes were cut in top for a self-rimming sink and deck-mounted fittings; plumbing runs through false drawer.

# ■ Storage solutions

**Glass display shelves** bring a touch of elegance and openness to a tiny powder room layout. Triple-thick, laminated shelves are supported discreetly at three points; recess saves space.

**For watching soaps** in the suds, television is built into a bathroom wall. Above, cubbyholes hold electronic gear. Ventilation is provided from behind.

ARCHITECT: WARD SEYMOUR

**Square footage stolen** from an unfinished portion of the attic added open storage, a usable countertop, and light to what was a cramped, windowless bath.

ARCHITECT: KEN TATE

**Spare on parts,** yet full of style, this unadorned bath gives a salute to older homes built before spa tubs and multiple vanities. A simple floating shelf above the pedestal sink keeps the necessities handy.

# PLANNING GUIDELINES

## Decision-making ▪ Design ▪ Floor plans ▪ Products

The hallmark of today's bathrooms is style; it can be found in elegant powder rooms, gracious guest baths, efficient family bathrooms, and spacious master suites. Inspired by innovative designs, fashionable fixtures and fittings, and a refreshing palette of colors, the zest for home decorating has progressed to the bathroom from other parts of the house. The introduction of new products and materials—stylish yet durable—has added momentum.

But changes in lifestyle and the economy are at the heart of the bathroom remodeling trend. More and more people are deciding to make the most of the home they already own, rather than move to another one. And in the process they're changing the face of the bathroom. Not long ago, the standard bath was simply a room with utilitarian fixtures. Today's bathroom serves many needs. At its best, it can be a sanctuary from the busy world and a place to pamper yourself.

Planning your new bathroom can be one of the most enjoyable aspects of remodeling; it's the first step toward creating the kind of room you want. In this chapter, you'll learn about bathroom planning, from evaluating your existing bathroom to drawing floor plans for a new one, and determining the best ways to launch your project. The varied choices in fixtures, fittings, and materials are discussed in the "Bathroom showcase" (pages 54–63).

**In the master bath,** this spacious spa tub trimmed in marble connects a pair of his-and-her dressing and vanity areas. The polished brass fittings include a European-style hand shower.

# Getting started

"Where do I begin?" is one of the most-asked questions about remodeling. The answer is to start with an inventory of your existing bathroom. Once you've assessed the room's current condition and developed some remodeling goals, it will be easier to uncover the room's potential for greater comfort, more convenience, and better appearance.

To decide on your primary goals, complete the inventory below. List all the improvements you'd like to make in their order of importance. To make it easier to establish priorities, you can assign a numerical rating to each improvement or designate each as "must do" or "would like to do." The finished list will help you keep your remodeling goals in focus and guide you in setting a budget, working with professionals, and selecting products and materials.

Trends come and go, and the bathroom is not immune to changing fashion. Perhaps it's time to pull the plug on those outdated fixtures, surface treatments, colors, and accessories. Or you may decide to keep your fixtures and tile and redecorate around them with new paint and wallpaper; this approach can be a surprisingly effective and inexpensive way to update a room's appearance.

To help guide your decisions, start collecting ideas. Study the color photographs in this book. Let

## A BATHROOM INVENTORY

To analyze your present bathroom, take the bathroom inventory that follows—it's one of the most important tools in designing your new bathroom. Think of this exercise as a fact-finding process in which you identify specific conditions you'd like to improve, evaluate strengths and weaknesses, and set goals for remodeling.

First, look at the surfaces. Would the bathroom's style be improved if you changed the walls, floor, ceiling, countertops, or cabinetry? Do your doors and drawers need new hardware? Would new windows, a new bathtub, or a new shower door improve the room?

But don't stop when you've examined those relatively superficial elements. Move on to the fundamentals of the room and everything in it—and the way it all works (or fails to work) for the people who use it.

**Layout.** Consider the following questions in relation to your bathroom's layout: Does the door open into the room? If so, can it inconvenience someone inside? When open, do cabinet or vanity doors and drawers block the door? Can two people use the sink or vanity area at the same time? Would your family benefit from the added privacy of a compartmentalized bathroom, with tub, shower, or toilet separate from each other and from the vanity? Is there ample room for toweling dry without hitting elbows? Are stored items within easy reach?

**Fixtures and fittings.** Before you rush out to buy new fixtures and fittings, consider whether the existing ones can be cleaned, refinished, or repaired. If not, decide what features you like and dislike about your current equipment. Are you pleased with the sizes, shapes, and materials? Are the faucets easy to turn on and off? Can you adjust water temperature for the sink and shower as easily as you'd like? Are you content with a bathtub, or would you like a shower also? Would you like to add a whirlpool bath?

**Walls, floor, and ceiling.** Moisture is the enemy of most room surfaces and subsurfaces and can be a particular problem in bathrooms. Water warps flooring, deteriorates paint, and wilts wallpaper. Examine the surfaces in your present bathroom for chips, cracks, bubbles, mold, mildew, and other maladies. Is your tile uneven? Are the grout and caulking in good condition? Have any subsurfaces been damaged by excess moisture?

If any of your surfaces are in poor condition or you want to make a decorative change, be sure to consider moisture-resistance, maintenance, and durability when you choose new materials. The choices in color, pattern, texture, and style are enormous.

**Countertops.** Do you have ample counter space in your bathroom? If not, decide where you need more room for storage or display, or simply for a convenient place to put things down. Are existing countertops in good condition? Are joints and corners easy to keep clean? Would you prefer a different type of countertop material, or has the present material been satisfactory?

**Storage.** Before you think about increasing your storage capacity, clean out and organize your bathroom's existing storage areas. If you're still short of space, determine your most pressing storage needs. Would you like a recessed medicine cabinet, better storage for cleaning supplies, a place for dirty laundry, or a tilt-out bin to hold your bathroom scale? Consider adding a vanity, wall cabinets, or even a floor-to-ceiling unit complete with shelves and bins. Can you enlarge the room to gain space? Is it possible to store some items in a hall closet or other nearby space?

**Lighting.** Old bathrooms rarely have enough properly placed light fixtures. If your bathroom has only one overhead light or a single fixture above the medicine cabi-

them spur your imagination—you're almost certain to find many ideas that you'd like to adapt to your own setting.

Turn, too, to the showcase on pages 54–63, where various types of fixtures and fittings are illustrated and described. Peruse magazines and tour model homes in your neighborhood.

To collect more ideas and get a closer look at new products, visit showrooms and stores displaying bathroom fixtures, cabinetry, light fixtures, wall coverings, tile, and flooring products. As you shop around, try to identify what you like about certain styles. You can obtain catalogues, brochures, and color charts from stores and from manufacturers. Seek out helpful salespersons and ask questions about products that interest you. The answers and advice you receive can be invaluable.

As you accumulate notes, clippings, photographs, and brochures, file your remodeling ideas in a notebook. Choose a binder with several divisions or file your material in separate 9 by 12-inch envelopes. Organize by subjects, such as best overall style, layouts and plans, pleasing color combinations, fixtures and fittings, lighting, and accessory ideas. Then review your remodeling goals and adapt the categories to suit your project.

---

net, you'll certainly want to give some thought to improving the room's artificial lighting. In additional to upgrading general lighting, would you like to add task lighting? Are you pleased with the appearance of existing light fixtures, and is the kind of light (fluorescent or incandescent) what you want? Consider bringing in more natural light. You can do this by adding a skylight, enlarging an existing window, or creating a new window.

**Electrical outlets and switches.** Note the location and number of electrical outlets and switches. Are there enough outlets? Are switches and outlets conveniently placed? If you need more electrical outlets, you may want to replace a single outlet with a double one. Plan to substitute circuit-breaking GFCI outlets for standard plugs in all wet areas in the bathroom. For greater convenience in a large space, you can install two and three-way switches for lights.

**Heating and ventilation.** Basic for bathroom comfort are a controlled temperature and good ventilation. No one enjoys the shock of a chilly bathroom on a cold morning. In a poorly ventilated bathroom, you may gasp for air in the middle of a steamy shower or have to stop to wipe off a foggy mirror while shaving. Note any problems caused by poor heating or ventilation, and don't overlook the problem of mold or mildew.

**Water and energy conservation.** Heating the bathroom and heating water consume a lot of energy. Are the water heater, pipes, and walls well insulated? Is the shower head equipped with a flow restrictor or shut-off valve? If you plan to buy a new toilet, have you considered a water-saving model?

**Privacy.** Does the door or window of your bathroom open to a public area? If so, you may want to consider relocating the opening or designing special window or exterior treatments to increase privacy. You should also check your bathroom for uninsulated pipes, finishing materials that reflect sound, and insufficient floor, wall, or ceiling insulation.

**Accessories.** Make a list of your bathroom accessories and note any additions or deletions you'd like to make, as well as any changes you want in quality, quantity, or style. Perhaps you'd like to replace mismatched towel bars and other accessories with a coordinated collection in glass, ceramic, or brightly colored plastic. Do you want the finish on towel bars, mirror frames, and cabinet hardware to match existing or new fittings? Also, look at your towels; aside from being functional, do they complement the room's color scheme? Do you have sufficient towel bars, and are they conveniently placed?

**Maintenance.** Some bathrooms are easier to maintain than others. Evaluate your bathroom's trouble spots, such as soap buildup, discolored grout, and streaked walls. In planning your project, consider installing smooth, seamless or jointless materials (except flooring) and ones especially designed to withstand moisture. If your fixtures are difficult to clean, you may want to refinish or replace them.

**Family needs.** A bathroom should be easy for everyone to use. Take time to consider the special needs of family members and regular visitors, including children and elderly or disabled persons. Can an adult bathe a small child safely and comfortably? Is the tub and/or shower equipped with a nonskid base and grab bars? If wheelchair access is a consideration, is the entry wide enough, and is there ample space for easy turning? Can all the fixtures be used without assistance? For more information on barrier-free baths, see page 43.

# Your present plan

You've taken a critical look at your bathroom, analyzing its good points and noting where you want to make improvements. If your goals point to simple redecorating or minor remodeling, skip ahead to the design information beginning on page 48 and the "Bathroom showcase" on pages 54–63 for help.

For more ambitious remodeling plans, you'll need to measure the room and draw it to scale. The process of measuring the bathroom elements and perimeter will increase your awareness of the existing space. Scale drawings also serve as a foundation for future design and may satisfy the permit requirements of your local building department. Such plans will also help you communicate your ideas to any professional you hire.

The information here will tell you how to measure your bathroom, record those measurements, and draw a two-dimensional floor plan to scale. You'll also learn how to make elevation drawings of each wall.

## Measuring the room

Before you begin taking measurements, draw a rough sketch of the bathroom, its various elements, and any adjacent areas that may be included in the remodeling. Make the sketch as large as the paper allows so you'll have ample room to write in the dimensions. Note any suspected deviations from the standard wall and partition thickness (usually about 5 inches). The sketch should also show all projections, recesses, windows, doors, and door swings.

**Tools.** Listed below are some tools and supplies that will help you with your measuring and drawing tasks. You can find these tools at hardware, stationery, and art supply stores.

- Retractable steel measuring tape or folding wooden rule
- Ruler or T-square
- Triangle
- Compass
- Graph paper (four squares to an inch)
- Tracing paper
- Masking tape
- Pencils
- Eraser
- Clipboard or pad with 8½ by 11-inch paper

**How to measure.** It's important to record the dimensions on the sketch as you measure, using feet and inches as an architect would (you may also want to translate certain dimensions, such as those for tubs and shower enclosures, to inches). Measure to the nearest ⅛ inch, since even a fraction of an inch counts in fitting and spacing bathroom elements. All mea-surements should be taken to the wall, not to projecting wood trim or baseboards.

First, measure the room's dimensions—the floor, ceiling, and walls; measure each wall at counter height. To find out if the bathroom is square, measure the diagonals (corner to opposite corner). Don't worry if the room isn't square; just be sure your drawing reflects any irregularities.

With the overall dimensions recorded on your sketch, measure the fixtures and other elements in the room and the distances between them, and add this information to your sketch. You can use a wall-by-wall approach, or you can measure by category: fixtures, doors, windows, cabinetry, shelves, and accessories.

Depending on the extent of your remodeling goals, your sketch could include locations of the following: load-bearing walls and partitions, electrical outlets and switches, light fixtures, drains, pipes, and vents. If you want to enlarge your bathroom—or just add more storage space—show relevant adjacent hall space, closets, rooms, and outdoor areas that you may be able to incorporate.

Note any heights that may affect your remodeling plans. These might include the clearance space under a duct or sloping ceiling, the floor-to-ceiling height, and the distance from the floor to the tops and bottoms of the windows.

## Drawing to scale

The secrets to drawing a useful floor plan and elevations are a well-prepared sketch with accurate measurements and a reasonable amount of skill at converting those measurements to the scale you choose. Your drawings don't have to be works of art, but they should be precise, complete, and easy to read.

Though architects sometimes use a ¼-inch scale (¼ inch equals 1 foot), using a ½-inch scale for your bathroom remodeling drawings is easier, especially when you want to include all the elements of the room and write their dimensions.

**How to draw floor plans.** With masking tape, attach the corners of the graph paper to a smooth working surface. Use a ruler, T-square, or triangle to draw all horizontal and vertical lines; make right angles exact. Use a compass to indicate door swings.

To complete the floor plan, refer to your sketch and the sample finished floor plan on the facing page. Indicating walls and partitions by dark, thick lines will make the floor plan easier to read.

**How to draw elevations.** Elevations, or straight-on views of each bathroom wall, show the visual pattern created by all the elements against that wall. Sketch the elements on each wall, measure carefully, and record the figures as you did for the floor plan; then redraw your elevation sketches on graph paper.

## SAMPLE FLOOR PLAN & ELEVATION

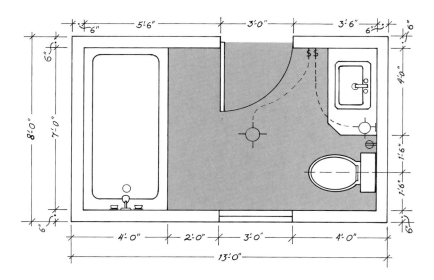

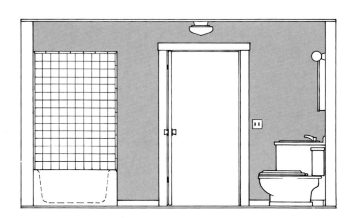

**The drawings** of your existing bathroom should look like the floor plan above and the elevation sketch at right. Be sure to add the appropriate architectural symbols to your floor plan to indicate outlets, switches, windows, and light fixtures.

# ARCHITECTURAL SYMBOLS

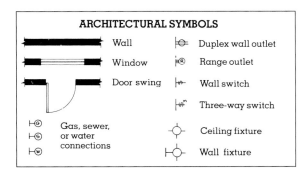

### ARCHITECTURAL SYMBOLS

| | | | |
|---|---|---|---|
| ▬▬▬ | Wall | ⊖ | Duplex wall outlet |
| ▭ | Window | ® | Range outlet |
| ⌐ | Door swing | ↗ | Wall switch |
| | | ↗₃ | Three-way switch |
| ⊢Ⓖ | Gas, sewer, | | |
| ⊢Ⓢ | or water | ⊝ | Ceiling fixture |
| ⊢Ⓦ | connections | ⊢⊝ | Wall fixture |

Architects and designers use a set of standard symbols to indicate certain features on floor plans; some of the most common ones are shown at left. It's a good idea to become familiar with these symbols, since you'll want to use them on your own plans. Also, you'll need to know them to communicate with your building department, contractor, or designer.

# Basic layouts

Once you've analyzed your present bathroom's assets and liabilities, it's time to start planning your new one. While brainstorming, try to have some basic layout schemes in mind. The floor plans shown below provide a starting point. Keep in mind that these layouts can be combined, adapted, and expanded to meet your needs. For additional ideas, study the photos on pages 6–35.

The "best" bathroom layout doesn't exist—good layouts vary dramatically. Generally, though, a workable floor plan provides for good access to the room, easy movement within the room, and the convenient use of fixtures and storage units.

Here are some layout guidelines categorized by type of bathroom.

**Powder room.** This two-fixture room, also known as a guest bath or half-bath, contains a toilet and a sink and perhaps some limited storage space. Fixtures can be placed side by side or on opposite or even adjacent walls, depending on the shape of the room. Very small sinks are available for extra-tight spaces.

Because the guest bathroom is used only occasionally and for short intervals of time, it's a good place to enjoy more decorative but perhaps less durable finishes, such as brass, copper, and upholstery. The door should swing open against a wall, clear of any fixtures. Where space is tight, a pocket door may be the ideal solution.

Consideration should be given to privacy. Preferably, a guest bath should open off a hallway, not directly into the living room, family room, or dining area.

**Family bath.** The family bath usually contains three fixtures—a toilet, a sink, and a bathtub or shower or combination tub/shower. The fixture arrangement varies, depending on the size and shape of the room. (Several configurations are shown below.) Family baths often have cluster or corridor layouts; they should be at least 5 feet by 7 feet.

To enable several family members to use the bathroom at the same time, consider putting in two sinks. Another possible solution is compartmentalizing, or separating fixture areas. One common arrangement is to isolate the toilet and shower from the sink and grooming area. This configuration can work well to increase privacy when it's not feasible to add a new bathroom.

The family bath is one of the most frequently used rooms in the house. Therefore, be sure to choose durable, moisture-resistant, easy-to-clean fixtures and finishes. Also, be sure to plan adequate storage space for each user's needs.

## SAMPLE BATHROOM LAYOUTS

**POWDER ROOM**
4' by 4'-6"

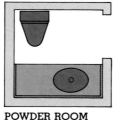

**POWDER ROOM**
5' by 5'

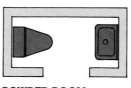

**POWDER ROOM**
3' by 6'

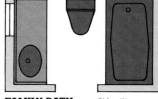

**FAMILY BATH**  5' by 7'

**FAMILY BATH**  7' by 11'

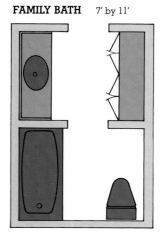

**FAMILY BATH**
8' by 12'

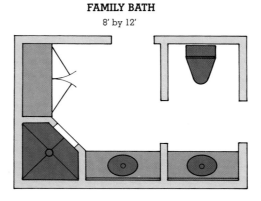

**BACK-TO-BACK**  5' by 7' each

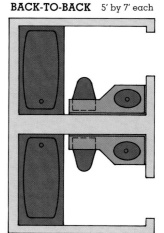

**Children's bath.** Ideally, this bathroom is located between two bedrooms used by children, so there's direct access from each room.

If there's space, you may want to consider shared bathing and toilet facilities and an individual sink and dressing area for each child. When several children are sharing one bath, color coding of drawers, towel hooks, and other storage areas can help minimize territorial battles.

Children's baths require special attention to safety and maintenance. Single-lever faucets reduce the chances of a hot-water burn; slip-resistant surfaces prevent accidents. A timer on the light switch keeps your electrical bill down. Plastic laminate countertops and cabinets are a good choice—they're durable and easy to clean. For more information on safety in the bathroom, turn to page 47.

**Master bath suite.** The master bath has become more than just a place to grab a quick shower and run a comb through your hair. No longer merely a utilitarian space, today's master bath reflects the personality and interests of its owners. Often, it includes dressing and grooming areas, toilet and bathing facilities, and such other amenities as fireplaces, whirlpool baths, oversize tubs, and bidets. Outside this bath is a natural place for a spa, sunbathing deck, or private garden.

Here are some "extras" that you may want to consider for your master bath. Make sure that you provide adequate ventilation to prevent water damage (from splashes and condensation) to delicate objects and equipment.

■ Walk-in dressing room

■ Exercise room

■ Makeup center

■ Reading nook

■ Home entertainment center

■ Art gallery

■ Greenhouse or sun room

**Barrier-free bath.** If you're remodeling to accommodate a disabled or elderly person, be sure you're aware of that person's special needs. Different heights, clearances, and room dimensions may be required. For example, to accommodate a wheelchair, the room must have specific clearances (see page 45). The door should swing out to allow easy movement in and out of the room. The shower needs to be curbless so a wheelchair can roll in unobstructed. You may also want to install grab bars, use levers in place of round door knobs, and choose fixtures and fittings specifically designed for the disabled.

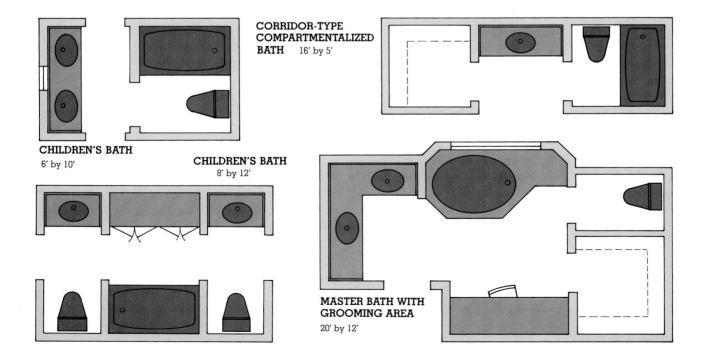

**CORRIDOR-TYPE COMPARTMENTALIZED BATH**   16' by 5'

**CHILDREN'S BATH**
6' by 10'

**CHILDREN'S BATH**
8' by 12'

**MASTER BATH WITH GROOMING AREA**
20' by 12'

**MINIMUM CLEARANCES**

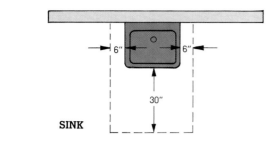

SINK

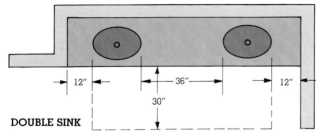

DOUBLE SINK

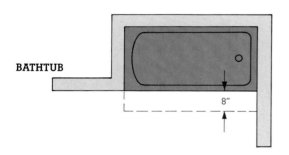

BATHTUB

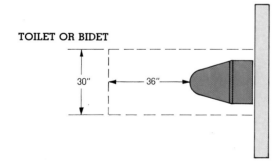

TOILET OR BIDET

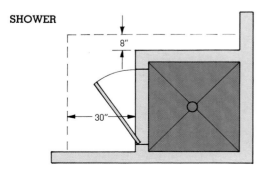

SHOWER

# Locating fixtures

Before you can actually plan your bathroom layout and place your fixtures, it's important to understand some basic facts about plumbing lines, minimum heights and clearances, and fixture location. Only then can you plan a layout that makes sense both structurally and economically.

Once you have all the facts at hand, you'll be ready to experiment with layouts. To do this, trace the scale floor plan of your existing bathroom, including any adjoining space you're planning to "borrow." If you're considering removing or relocating walls, eliminate those existing partitions. As you experiment with different arrangements, set aside any plans you like and start fresh with another tracing of the bathroom's perimeter in its future form.

One of the biggest challenges in designing layouts for your new bathroom is keeping track of your ideas. If they're flowing, you won't want to forget your best inspirations just because you didn't get them down on paper.

One answer is to move paper cutouts around your floor plan and then sketch the best plans you devise with them. To use this method, first draw the perimeter of your existing floor plan and any adjacent areas to be included in the project. Then, using graph paper, make cutouts (to scale) of fixtures, cabinets, countertops, and other elements—both existing features you plan to keep and new ones to be added. Move the cutouts around the floor plan; when you hit on a layout you like, sketch it so you'll have a record of it. When you think you've exhausted the possibilities, compare the plans and evaluate them.

## The existing structure

You'll keep costs down and simplify construction if you select a layout that uses the existing water supply, drain lines, and vent stack. If that's not possible, you may want to study the how-to section beginning on page 65 to familiarize yourself with the work that plumbing, wiring, and structural changes entail.

If you're adding on to your house, try to locate the new bathroom near an existing bathroom or near the kitchen. It's also more economical to arrange fixtures against one or two walls, eliminating the need for additional plumbing lines.

Generally, you can move a sink a few inches from its present position with only minor plumbing changes. Your existing supply and drain lines can usually support a second sink. You can extend existing supply and drain lines if the distance from the vent is less than the maximum distance allowed by your local code; if not, you'll have to install a secondary vent—a major undertaking.

If your bathroom has a wood floor with a crawlspace, basement, or first floor underneath, it's relatively simple to move both plumbing and wiring. But in rooms with concrete floors, it's an expensive proposition to move plumbing or wiring that's located under the concrete. To gain access to the lines, you would have to go through the laborious process of breaking up and removing the concrete.

Structural changes, especially those entailing work on load-bearing walls, fall into the category of serious remodeling and may require professional help. Relocating a door or window opening may also involve a lot of work, including framing and finishing. Adding a partition wall, on the other hand, is an easier and less expensive job.

## Heights & clearances

Building codes specify minimum required clearances between, beside, and in front of bathroom fixtures to allow adequate room for use, cleaning, and repair. To help in your initial planning, check the minimum clearances shown on the facing page.

Generally, you can locate side-by-side fixtures closer together than fixtures positioned opposite each other. If a sink is opposite a bathtub or toilet, keep a minimum of 30 inches between them. Children, elderly, and disabled persons may require assistance or special fixtures; if you anticipate such needs, allow extra space in your layout.

Shown above, at right, are standard heights for countertops, shower heads, and accessories. If you and others using the bathroom are especially tall or short, you may wish to customize the room to your own requirements. However, when planning such a change, keep one eye on your home's resale value: will potential buyers find these alterations as convenient as you do?

Basic height and clearance guidelines for a barrier-free space are illustrated at right. For additional help, look for an architect or designer who specializes in this expanding field.

## Fixture arrangement

It's usually best to position the largest unit—the bathtub or shower—first. Be sure you allow space for convenient access, for cleaning, and, if needed, for bathing a child.

Next, place the sink (or sinks). The most frequently used fixture in the bathroom, the sink should be positioned out of the traffic pattern. Be sure to plan for ample room in front for reaching below the sink and give plenty of elbow room at the sides.

Locate the toilet (and bidet, if you have one) away from the door; often, the toilet is placed beside the tub or shower. A toilet and bidet should be positioned next to each other.

Don't forget about the swing-radius for windows and doors. To resolve a conflict, you could either reverse a standard door's hardware from left to right or substitute a pocket door.

## STANDARD HEIGHTS

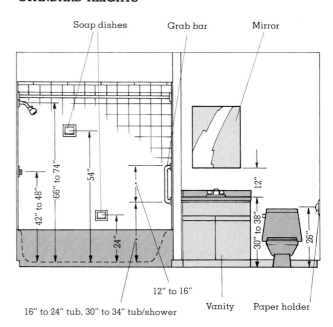

Soap dishes   Grab bar   Mirror

42" to 48"   66" to 74"   54"   24"   30" to 38"   12"   26"

16" to 24" tub, 30" to 34" tub/shower

12" to 16"   Vanity   Paper holder

## BARRIER-FREE GUIDELINES

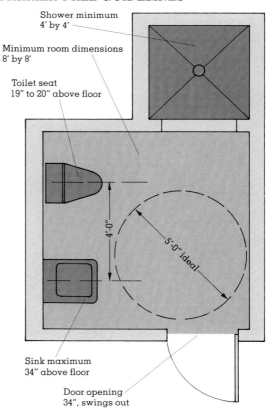

Shower minimum 4' by 4'

Minimum room dimensions 8' by 8'

Toilet seat 19" to 20" above floor

4'-0"   5'-0" ideal

Sink maximum 34" above floor

Door opening 34", swings out

# Finishing touches

Once you've decided on a basic layout and marked the design you've worked out onto a clean tracing of your bathroom's floor plan, you can turn your attention to the walls. Begin by drawing an elevation of each wall and marking on those elevations the fixtures you've already located. Then you'll be ready to add all the other elements that go into your bathroom: storage, mirrors, towel bars, amenities, and heating and ventilation details.

To do this, you can use the same cutout technique you used for the fixtures (see page 44). But now you'll be working on an elevation, not a floor plan, and you'll be preparing a different set of cutouts—straight-on views of fixtures, cabinets, mirrors, and other elements. Arrange these cutouts with an eye for line, shape, and scale (see page 48). The plans you sketch as you move the cutouts around will help you visualize the room as a whole and see relationships between horizontal, vertical, diagonal, and curved lines. Be sure to set aside sketches of the arrangements you like so you can compare them later.

## Storage needs

After arranging the fixtures, plan your storage space. Consider what you need to store, how much space you need for it, and how best to organize the space. If you're planning to expand your storage capacity, review your notes from the inventory to pinpoint which items require space.

Consider equipping a vanity or cabinet with racks, shelves, pull-outs, or lazy susans for supplies.

Many bathroom items are candidates for open storage—why not display colorful towels or stacks of soap on open shelving? For a look at a variety of successful storage solutions, see pages 30–35.

## Filling in the details

Choosing appropriate fixtures, fittings, and cabinetry will block out your bathroom plan quickly, but don't forget the finishing touches that make or break a handsome, comfortable design. Below, you'll find a checklist of bathroom amenities to consider.

**Surfaces.** Floor, wall, and countertop surfaces should be durable as well as attractive. For details about the characteristics of the various surface materials, including plastic laminate, solid-surface, wood, stone, and tile, see pages 55 and 62–63 in the section "Bathroom showcase."

**Saunas and steam showers.** These luxurious features, once found mainly in gyms and health clubs, have recently entered the residential bathroom.

A sauna is a small, wood-lined room (often sold prefabricated) that heats itself to around 200°F. In addition to insulated walls, a solid-core door, and double-paned glass (if any), you'll also need an electric or gas sauna heater. Minimum size for a sauna is about 65 cubic feet per person. But don't make the space overly large—you'll just have more space to heat.

New steam units are small enough to be housed in any number of convenient locations—inside a stor-

ARCHITECT: REMICK ASSOCIATES

**Heated towel bars** keep bath linens toasty and also serve as radiators. Brass rack harnesses old-fashioned hydronic heat; you can also buy electric versions.

# PLAYING IT SAFE IN THE BATHROOM

About 25 percent of all home accidents occur in the bathroom. You can reduce the risk of injury by careful planning and by encouraging safe practices. Here are some guidelines.

■ Install sufficient lighting. Include a night-light, especially if you have small children.

■ Choose tempered glass, plastic, and other shatter-proof materials for construction and accessories.

■ Install locks that can be opened from the outside in an emergency.

■ Locate clothes hooks above eye level.

■ Select a tub or shower with a nonslip surface. For existing fixtures, use a rubber bath mat.

■ Install L-shaped or horizontal grab bars, capable of supporting a person weighing 250 pounds, in tub and shower areas. Installation must be done properly—bracing between studs may be required. Plaster-mounted accessories don't provide sufficient support.

■ Anchor any carpeting. Choose area rugs or bath mats with nonskid backing.

■ Avoid scalding by lowering the setting of your water heater or by installing a temperature-limiting mixing valve or a pressure-balancing valve to prevent sudden temperature drops.

■ Test the water temperature before stepping into a shower or tub and when assisting a child or elderly person. Place shower controls where they can be accessed quickly and conveniently.

■ Be sure electrical outlets are grounded and protected with GFCI circuit breakers. Outlets should be out of reach from the shower or bathtub. Install safety covers over unused outlets.

■ Avoid using electrical appliances in wet areas. Keep portable heaters out of the bathroom.

■ If children live in or visit your house, buy medicines (and, when possible, household cleansers) in child-proof containers. Store these items in a cabinet equipped with a safety latch. Tape seldom-used non-safety containers closed. Check the contents of your medicine cabinet at least twice a year and discard outdated medicines and those with unreadable or incomplete directions.

■ Keep a first aid kit handy for use in an emergency. Post phone numbers of the nearest emergency rescue unit and poison control center.

---

age cabinet, in an adjacent closet or alcove, or in a tall crawlspace. Besides the steam box, all you need is an airtight shower door, a comfortable bench, and effective ventilation.

**Lighting.** Don't leave lighting as an afterthought; it should be part of the initial design. A wide range of incandescent, fluorescent, and halogen light sources are on the market today, as well as a huge selection of fixtures to house them.

Design ideas for both natural and artificial light appear on pages 50–51. For a look at how light can be used in bathrooms, see pages 24–29.

**Electrical outlets and switches.** Tentatively mark the locations of outlets and switches. Every countertop longer than 12 inches should have a two-plug outlet; every wall must have an outlet every 12 feet—or at least one outlet per wall, regardless of size. Be sure that outlets within 6 feet of any wet area are grounded and protected with GFCI circuit breakers.

Switches are usually placed 44 inches above the floor on the open (or latch) side of doorways.

**Hardware and accessories.** Think now about how you'll coordinate doorknobs, drawer pulls, towel bars, a toilet-paper holder, and other accessories with your fixtures, fittings, and surfaces. Aim for an integrated overall look.

## Heating & ventilation

If you want to extend your existing heating system to a new bathroom, check with a professional to be sure your system can handle the added load. You can relocate a hot air register in the floor or in the vanity kickspace by changing the duct work beneath the floor; ducts for wall registers can be rerouted in the stud wall. If you're adding a register, locate it where the duct work can be extended easily from the existing system and where you won't sacrifice wall space.

Hot air duct work is best done by a heating or sheet metal contractor. Extending hot water or steam systems is easier, but it, too, calls for professional help. It may be more practical to equip your bathroom with an electric space heater, which can be recessed in the wall or ceiling, or with an electric heat lamp.

Local building codes may require exhaust fans in certain bathrooms and specify their placement; check the code before you complete your design. Such fans are relatively simple to add or relocate. These units are installed in the ceiling between joists or in the wall between studs, and may require duct work to the outside.

# Line, shape & scale

It may never occur to you to consider line, shape, and scale when you draw up your plans. Yet these design elements hold the key to a balanced, visually pleasing design. Take another look at your bathroom elevation sketches to examine these elements. You may want to improve the existing conditions—or perhaps you'll decide to try an entirely new approach.

## Line—the dominant theme

Most bathrooms incorporate many different kinds of lines—vertical, horizontal, diagonal, curved, and angular. However, one line usually dominates and characterizes the design. Vertical lines give a sense of height, horizontals add width, diagonals suggest movement, and curved and angular lines impart a sense of grace and dynamism.

Repeating similar lines gives the room a sense of unity. Look at one of your elevation sketches. How do the vertical lines created by the cabinets, vanity, windows, doors, mirrors, and shower or tub unit fit together? Does the horizontal line marking the top of the window align with other horizontal lines in the room, such as the tops of the shower stall, door, and mirror? Clearly, not everything can or should line up perfectly, but the effect is far more pleasing if a number of elements are aligned, particularly when they're the highest features in the room.

## Shape—a sense of harmony

Continuity and compatibility in shape also contribute to a unified design. Of course, you needn't repeat the same shape throughout the room—carried too far, that becomes monotonous.

Study the shapes created by doorways, windows, countertops, fixtures, and other elements. Look at patterns in your flooring, wall covering, shower curtain, and towels. Are they different or similar? If they're different, do they clash? If they're similar, are they boring? Consider ways to complement existing shapes or add compatible new ones. For example, if there's an arch over a recessed bathtub, create an arch over a doorway or repeat the arch on the trim of a shelf.

## Scale—everything in proportion

When the scale of bathroom elements is in proportion to the overall size of the room, the design feels harmonious. A small bath seems even smaller if equipped with large fixtures and a large vanity. But the same bathroom appears larger, or at least in scale, when equipped with space-saving fixtures, a petite vanity, and open shelves,

Consider the proportions of adjacent features as well. When wall cabinets or linen shelves extend to the ceiling, they often make a room seem top-heavy—and therefore smaller. To counteract this look without losing storage space, place cabinet doors or shelves closer together at the top. Let your floor plan and elevation drawings suggest other ways you can modify the scale of different elements to improve your design.

ARCHITECT: REMICK ASSOCIATES

**Squares are everywhere,** but size and color contrast set surfaces apart. Easy-to-clean glazed tiles line walls to eye level. Floor mosaics set color accent and lead eye around corner, enlarging sense of space. Tile-high glass-block partition restates square motif and screens shower area while letting light pass through.

# Color, texture & pattern

The ways you use color, texture, and pattern play an important part in your design. After you narrow down your selections, make a sample board to see how your choices work together. Color charts for fixtures are readily available, as are paint chips, fabric swatches, and wallpaper and flooring samples.

## Choosing your colors

The size and orientation of your bathroom, your personal preferences, and the mood you want to create all affect color selection. Here are some color principles to guide you.

Light colors reflect light, making walls recede; thus, a small bathroom treated with light colors appears more spacious. Dark colors absorb light and can visually lower a ceiling or shorten a narrow room.

When considering colors for a small bathroom, remember that too much contrast has the same effect as a dark color: it reduces the sense of spaciousness. Contrasting colors work well for adding accents or drawing attention to interesting structural elements. But if you need to conceal a problem feature, it's best to use one color throughout the area.

Oranges, yellows, and other colors with a red tone impart a feeling of warmth to a room, but they also contract space. Cool colors—blues, greens, and colors with a blue tone—make an area seem larger. A light, monochromatic color scheme (using different shades of one color) is restful and serene. Contrasting colors add vibrancy and excitement to a design. But a color scheme with contrasting colors can be overpowering unless the tones of the colors are varied. Note, too, that the temperature and intensity of colors will be affected by lighting.

## Adding interest with texture & pattern

Texture and pattern work like color in defining a room's style and sense of space. The bathroom's surface materials may include many different textures, from a glossy countertop to smooth wood cabinets to a roughly surfaced quarry-tile floor.

Rough textures absorb light, make colors look duller, and lend a feeling of informality. Smooth textures reflect light and tend to suggest elegance or modernity. Using similar textures helps unify a design and create a mood.

Pattern choices must harmonize with the predominant style of the room. Though pattern is usually associated with wall coverings or a cabinet finish, even natural substances such as wood, brick, and stone create patterns.

While variation in texture and pattern adds interest, too much variety can be overstimulating. It's best to let a strong feature or dominant pattern be the focus of your design and choose other surfaces to complement rather than compete with it.

**Around the whirlpool tub,** V-groove paneling enhances the old-fashioned ambience of this new bathroom and provides a more water-friendly buffer between the tub and the wallpaper. Stock chair railing hung upside down caps off the paneling on the wall.

# Lighting guidelines

No matter how beautifully it's decorated, a room with inadequate lighting will be an unpleasant place to be—and difficult to use. In a multiple-use room such as a bathroom, the light levels required range from very soft ambient light to strong directional task lighting. Usually, you can achieve a pleasing level by bringing in natural light through windows and skylights and supplementing it with artificial lighting.

### Natural light

To bring natural light into your bathroom, you can use windows and doors (opening to secluded areas) as well as skylights—alone or in combination.

A single window in the middle of a wall often creates a glaring contrast with the surrounding area. To increase the amount of natural light, consider placing windows on adjacent walls or installing a skylight. Either will provide uniform lighting over a larger area. To maximize sunlight, position openings so they face south or west. But to avoid unwanted heat and glare, it's best to locate windows and skylights so they have a northern or eastern exposure.

Windows, available in many styles, may have frames of wood, aluminum, vinyl, or steel. All-vinyl windows and wood windows clad in vinyl or aluminum require the least maintenance.

Though you can have a skylight custom-made, many prefabricated units are available. Some open for ventilation. If there's a space between the ceiling and roof, you'll need a light shaft to direct light to the bathroom below. The shaft may be straight, angled, or splayed.

You can combine glass in different forms (panels and glass blocks, for example) and finishes (clear and translucent) to bring in light and view while still ensuring privacy. Generally, transparent materials are suitable above chin height of the tallest occupant. But be sure to check the heights and locations of neighbors' windows.

### Artificial lighting

Artificial lighting can be separated into three categories: task, ambient, and accent. Task lighting illuminates a particular area where a visual activity, such as shaving or applying makeup, takes place. Ambient, or general, lighting fills the undefined areas of a room with a soft level of light—enough, say, for a relaxing soak in a whirlpool tub. Accent lighting, which is primarily decorative, is used to highlight architectural features, set a mood, or provide drama.

**Which fixtures are best?** Generally speaking, lighting in a bathroom should be small and discreet. Consequently, recessed downlights are very popular. Fitted with the right baffle or shield, those fixtures alone can handle ambient, task, and accent needs.

In a larger bathroom, a separate fixture to light the shower or bath area—or any other distinct part in a compartmentalized design—may be needed. Shower fixtures should be waterproof units fitted with neoprene seals.

Fixtures around a makeup or shaving mirror should spread light over a person's face rather than onto the mirror surface. To avoid heavy shadows, place lights at the sides of the mirror, not just overhead. Wall sconces flanking the mirror not only provide light but also offer an opportunity for a stylish design statement.

And just for fun, why not consider decorative uplights in a soffit or strip lights in a kickspace area? These accents help provide a wash of ambient light and also serve as safe, pleasant night-lights.

Dimmers (also called rheostats) enable you to set a fixture at any level from a soft glow to a radiant brightness. They're also energy savers. It's easy and inexpensive to put incandescent bulbs on dimmers. The initial cost of dimmers for fluorescent lights is greater than for incandescents, and the variety of fixtures with dimmers is limited.

**Light bulbs and tubes.** Light sources can be grouped in general categories according to the way they produce light.

*Incandescent* light, the kind used most frequently in homes, is produced by a tungsten thread that burns slowly inside a glass tube. A-bulbs are the old standbys; R and PAR bulbs produce a more controlled beam; silvered-bowl types diffuse light. A number of decorative bulbs are also available.

Low-voltage incandescent lights are especially useful for accent lighting. Operating on 12 or 24 volts, these lights require transformers (which are often built into the fixtures) to step down the voltage from standard 120-volt household circuits.

*Fluorescent* tubes are unrivaled for energy efficiency; they also last far longer than incandescent bulbs. Older fluorescent tubes have been criticized for noise, flicker, and poor color rendition. Electronic ballasts and better fixture shielding against glare have remedied the first two problems; as for the last one, manufacturers have developed fluorescents in a wide spectrum of colors, from very warm (about 2,700 degrees K) to very cool (about 6,300 degrees K).

Bright, white *quartz halogen* bulbs are excellent for task lighting, pinpoint accenting, and other dramatic accents. Halogen is usually low-voltage but may be standard line current. The popular MR-16 bulb creates the tightest beam; for a longer reach and wider coverage, choose a PAR bulb. There's an abundance of smaller bulb shapes and sizes to fit pendants and undercabinet strip lights.

Halogen has two disadvantages: high initial cost and very high heat. Shop carefully—some fixtures on the market are not UL-approved.

ARCHITECT: MORIMOTO ARCHITECTS

**Multiple light sources** provide ambient, task, and accent light—day and night. Built-in sink fixture recessed behind "shoji-screen" trim spreads light via diffusing panels. Wall sconces add general light and decorative flair. A skylight brings in welcome sunshine.

**Contemporary pendants** follow lines of countertop and repeat in backsplash mirrors. Nonglare bulbs provide plenty of ambient and task light.

DESIGNER: OSBURN DESIGN

**Well-chosen accent lighting** adds pizzazz to a powder room. Diamond-patterned marble border is highlighted by hidden low-voltage strip lights.

ARCHITECT: J. ALLEN SAYLES

# Finalizing your plan

The planning process culminates with the drawing of your new floor plan. The floor plan is the basis for the remodeling work, for the preparation of a master list of products and materials, and for the acquisition of any necessary building permits.

### Drawing a floor plan

Draw the new floor plan in the same way as you did the existing floor plan (see pages 40–41). On the new plan, include both existing features you want to preserve and all proposed changes, such as new walls, partitions, doors, windows, skylights, light fixtures, electrical switches and outlets, fixtures, cabinets, countertops, and materials. If you prefer, you can hire a designer, drafter, or contractor to draw the final plan for you.

For more complicated projects, your local building department may require additional or more detailed drawings of structural, plumbing, and wiring changes. You may also need to show areas adjacent to the bathroom on the new plan so building officials can determine how the project will affect the rest of your house. Elevation sketches aren't required, but they'll serve as a helpful check in planning the work and ordering materials.

If you're the one ordering the materials for your remodeling project, you'll need to compile a detailed master list. Not only will this launch your work, but it will also help you keep track of purchases and deliveries. For each item that you plan to order, be sure to specify the following information: name and model or serial number, manufacturer, source of material, date of order, delivery date, color, size or dimensions, quantity, price (including tax and delivery charge), and second choice.

### Obtaining building permits

To discover which building codes may affect your remodeling project and whether a building permit is required, check with your city or county building department.

You probably won't need a building permit for simple jobs, such as replacing a window with one of the same size, installing a vanity, or changing floor or wall coverings. But for more substantial changes, you may need to apply for one or more of the following permits: structural, plumbing, mechanical heating or cooling, reroofing, or electrical. More complicated projects sometimes require that the design and the working drawings be executed by an architect, designer, or state-licensed contractor.

For your permit, you'll be charged either a flat fee or a percentage of the estimated cost of materials and labor. You may also have to pay a fee to have someone check the plans.

If you're acting as your own contractor, you must ask the building department to inspect the work as it progresses. (A professional contractor handles these inspections without your becoming involved.) The number of inspections depends on the complexity of the job. Failure to obtain a permit or an inspection may result in your having to dismantle completed work.

**NEW FLOOR PLAN**

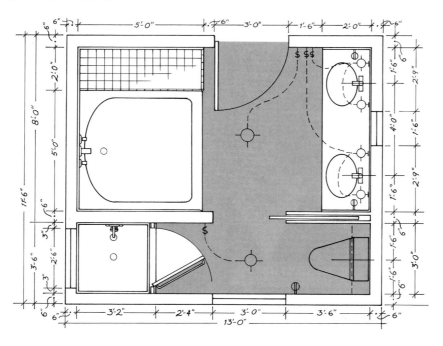

**In this redesign** of the floor plan shown on page 41, there's one big change: the lower, or outside, wall has been pushed out about 3 feet to house a new shower and toilet alcove. A pocket door seals this space, providing privacy while a second person uses the sink or tub areas.

New fixtures include a 5 by 5-foot platform tub and a second deck-mount sink. New light fixtures and electrical outlets complete the plan.

This project would require a professional to prepare detailed drawings of structural, plumbing, and wiring changes. If your project is less complicated, you could probably draw in all the changes yourself. A key to architectural symbols appears on page 41.

# WORKING WITH PROFESSIONALS

Major home remodeling projects are not easy work. If you know how to draw plans but dislike physical labor, you'll need someone else to perform the actual work. If you're able to wield a saw and hammer but can't draw a straight line, you may need professional help to prepare the new floor plan or specifications. Some people do the nonspecialized work, such as clearing the site and cleaning up later, but hire experts for everything else. Others let professionals handle the entire project—from drawing plans through applying the finishing touches.

No matter whom you consult, be as precise as possible about what you want and about your budget. Collect pertinent photographs, manufacturer's brochures, and advertisements. Describe the materials, fixtures, and fittings you want to use. Provide your preliminary plans and a rough figure of how much you plan to spend. If you have questions, write them down as you think of them. The more information you can supply and the more informed you are, the better job a professional will be able to do.

## Architect or designer?

Either an architect or a designer can draw plans acceptable to building department officials. Each can send out bids, help you select a contractor, and supervise the contractor's work to ensure that your plans and time schedule are being followed. Some architects and designers even double as their own contractors.

Most states do not require designers to be licensed, as architects must be; designers may charge less for their labor. If stress calculations must be made, designers need state-licensed engineers to design the structure and sign the working drawings; architects can do their own calculations.

Many architects are members of the American Institute of Architects (AIA), and many designers belong to the American Institute of Building Designers (AIBD). If you want to work with a bathroom designer, look for members of the National Kitchen & Bath Association (NKBA) or a Certified Bathroom Designer (CBD). Each association has a code of ethics and sponsors continuing programs to inform members about the latest building materials and techniques.

You may also wish to call on the services of an interior designer for finishing touches. These experts specialize in the decorating and furnishing of rooms. They can offer fresh, innovative ideas and advice. Through their contacts, you have access to materials and products not available at the retail level. Many designers belong to the American Society of Interior Designers (ASID), a professional organization.

Architects and designers may charge for time spent in an exploratory interview. For plans, you'll probably be charged on an hourly basis. If you want an architect or designer to select the contractor and keep an eye on construction, plan to pay either an hourly rate or a percentage of the cost of materials and labor—15 to 25 percent is typical. Descriptions of the services to be performed and the amount of the charges should be stated in advance in writing to prevent expensive misunderstandings later on.

## Choosing a contractor

Contractors are responsible for construction and all building operations. Often, they're also skilled drafters, able to draw working plans acceptable to building department officials; they can also obtain the necessary building permits.

If you decide to use a contractor, ask architects, designers, and friends for recommendations. To compare bids for the actual construction, contact at least three state-licensed contractors; give each one either an exact description and sketches of the desired remodeling or plans and specifications prepared by an architect or designer. Include a detailed account of who will be responsible for what work.

Don't be tempted to make price your only criterion for selection; reliability, quality of work, and on-time performance are also important. Ask the contractors for the names and phone numbers of recent clients. Call several and ask them how they feel about the contractor; if you can, inspect the contractor's work. Ask for proof of liability insurance; also check bank and credit references to determine the contractor's financial responsibility.

Though some contractors may want a fee based on a percentage of the cost of materials and labor, it's usually wiser to insist on a fixed-price bid. This protects you against both an unexpected rise in the cost of materials (assuming that the contractor does the buying) and the chance that the work will take more time, adding to your labor costs. Many states limit the amount of "good faith" money that contractors can require before work begins.

## Hiring subcontractors

When you act as your own general contractor and put various parts of your project out to bid with subcontractors (plumbers, tile setters, and the like), you must use the same care you'd exercise in hiring a general contractor.

Check the references, financial resources, and insurance coverage of a number of subcontractors. Once you've received bids and chosen your subcontractor, work out a detailed contract for each job and carefully supervise all work.

# Bathroom showcase

On the following pages is a wonderland of products and materials for the bathroom. Here you can see and compare at a glance a sampling of styles, installation methods, functions, and materials. Though it's by no means exhaustive, this showcase provides the basic information you'll need as you sketch layouts, gather specifications for contracts or ordering, and develop a budget.

Recognizing the need to conserve resources, many manufacturers today offer a variety of water-saving toilets, faucets, shower heads, and hand-held shower attachments, with price and performance comparable to those of their conventional counterparts. These fixtures and fittings can reduce not only the amount of water used but also the amount of energy needed to heat that water.

## CABINETS

Today, as changing lifestyles find new expression and bathrooms become grooming centers, exercise gyms, and spas, storage needs and configurations are also changing. One or more base vanities may still form the backbone of the storage scheme, but bath storage areas have become more stylish, their design integrated with mirrors, sink, lighting, and backsplash treatment. Perhaps you'll wish to add a bank of wall cabinets, let built-ins form knee walls between use areas, or plan a floor-to-ceiling unit.

Traditional American cabinets mask the raw front edges of each box with a 1 by 2 faceframe. On European, or frameless, cabinets, a simple narrow trim strip covers raw edges; doors and drawers usually fit to within ¼ inch of each other, revealing a thin sliver of

trim. Door hinges are invisible. Thanks to absolute standardization of every component, frameless cabinets are unsurpassed in versatility.

You can purchase a vanity cabinet with or without countertop and sink. Some manufacturers produce modular cabinet and shelf units for use with their vanities; other units include laundry bins, medicine cabinets, and closets. Standard width is 30 inches, increasing at 3 or 6-inch intervals, but some are as narrow as 12 inches and as wide as 60 inches. Standard heights range from 28 to 36 inches; depths range up to 24 inches.

If you don't find what you're looking for in the bath department, take a look at kitchen units; the differences between cabinet lines are slowly disappearing.

## Styles

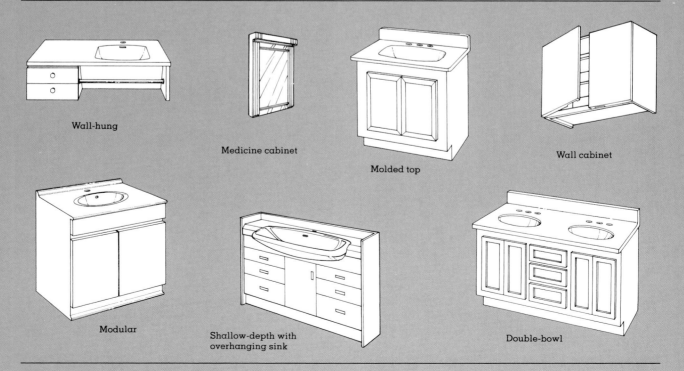

Wall-hung

Medicine cabinet

Molded top

Wall cabinet

Modular

Shallow-depth with overhanging sink

Double-bowl

# COUNTERTOPS

Plastic laminate, ceramic tile, solid-surface acrylic, and stone are the four major countertop materials currently in use. Synthetic marble, popular in the past, is losing ground to solid-surface materials. Wood is sometimes used for countertops, too, but the surface must be carefully sealed to prevent water damage.

| Style | Characteristics |
|---|---|
| **Plastic laminate** | Laminate comes in a wide range of colors, textures, and patterns. It's durable, easy to clean, water-resistant, and relatively inexpensive. However, it can scratch, scorch, chip, and stain. Also, smooth, reflective surfaces tend to show dirt and water marks. Conventional laminate has a dark backing that shows at its seams; new solid-color laminate, designed to avoid this, is somewhat brittle and more expensive. Post-formed tops, premolded and prefabricated, are the least expensive option; a custom top with built-up lip and backsplash looks best but is more costly. |
| **Ceramic tile** | Good-looking ceramic tile comes in many colors, textures, and patterns. Installed correctly, it's heatproof, scratch-resistant, and water-resistant. On the other hand, the grout may be hard to keep clean, even when a grout sealer is used. Also, tile's hard, irregular surface can chip delicate glass containers. High-gloss tiles show every smudge. Prices range from modest to extravagant, depending on style, accents, and accessory pieces. Nonporous glazed tiles won't soak up spills and stains. |
| **Solid-surface** | Durable, water-resistant, nonporous, and easy to clean, this marblelike material allows for a variety of edge details and sink installations, including integral units. Blemishes and scratches can be sanded out. Solid-surface countertops are expensive and require firm support from below. Until recently, color selection was limited to white, beige, and almond; now, imitation stone and pastels are readily available. Costs go up for wood inlays and other fancy edge details. |
| **Stone** | Granite and marble are beautiful natural materials for countertops. In most areas, you'll find a great selection of colors and figures. Stone is water-resistant, heatproof, easy to clean, and very durable. Oil, alcohol, and any acid (even chemicals in some water supplies) can stain marble and damage its high-gloss finish; granite can stand up to all of these. Solid stone slabs are very expensive. Stone tiles, including slate and limestone, are less expensive alternatives. |
| **Synthetic marble** | This group of man-made products, collectively known as "cast polymers," includes cultured marble, cultured onyx, and cultured granite. All three are relatively inexpensive and easy to clean. These products are often sold with an integral sink. Synthetic marble is not very durable, and scratches and dings are hard to mend (the surface finish is often only a thin veneer). Quality varies widely; look for Cultured Marble Institute or IAPMO certification. |
| **Wood** | Wood is handsome, natural, easily installed, and easy on grooming accessories and glass containers. However, wood is harder to keep clean than nonporous materials. If you use it in areas that will get wet (and that includes many bathroom surfaces), thoroughly protect it on all sides with a good sealer, such as polyurethane. Maple butcherblock, the most popular ready-made top, is sold in 24, 30, and 36-inch widths; installed price is comparable to ceramic or top-of-the-line laminate. Edge-joined oak, redwood, sugar pine, and teak are also used for counters. |

# SINKS

Sinks come in many shapes, sizes, colors, materials, and styles. The most commonly available styles are deck-mount, integral sink and countertop, pedestal, and wall-hung. Sinks have either no holes for fittings or holes for 4, 6, or 8-inch faucet assemblies; some also have holes for spray attachments and lotion dis-pensers (see page 59 for more about sink fittings). You'll find a wide selection of sink materials. Vitreous china, fiberglass-reinforced plastic, enameled cast iron, and enameled steel are the most common. Brass and copper sinks make striking accents, but they require zealous maintenance.

| Style | Characteristics |
|---|---|
| **Deck-mount, self-rimming** | A self-rimming sink has a molded overlap that's supported by the edge of the countertop cutout. The cutout is undersized, allowing the sink rim to sit on the countertop. This style is easy to install and offers the widest range in shapes, including shell, hexagon, and fluted. |
| **Deck-mount, flush** | A surrounding metal frame holds a flush-mount sink to the countertop. The frame comes in several finishes to match fittings. Keeping the joints between the frame, sink, and countertop clean requires some vigilance. This style is usually used with plastic laminate countertops. |
| **Deck-mount, unrimmed** | An unrimmed sink is recessed beneath the countertop opening and held in place by metal clips. Fittings are mounted through the countertop or directly on the sink. The sink-countertop joint requires a little extra effort to keep clean. This sink is a good choice for use with tile, plastic laminate, or synthetic marble countertops. |
| **Integral sink and countertop** | Made of solid-surface material, synthetic marble, vitreous china, or fiberglass, an integral sink and countertop has no joints, so installation and cleaning are easy. This one-piece molded unit sits on top of a vanity. Sink color can either match the countertop or complement it; edge-banding and other border options abound. Double-bowl units are available. |
| **Pedestal** | Pedestal sinks are making a big comeback. Typically made of vitreous china in a wide range of traditional and modern designs, these elegant sinks are easy to install. The pedestal usually hides the plumbing. Some models have old-style vanity legs. Pedestal sinks are generally among the highest-priced basins. There's no storage space beneath. |
| **Wall-hung** | Like pedestals, wall-hung sinks are enjoying a revival. Materials and styling are similar; in fact, some designs are available in either version. Generally speaking, these are the least expensive and most compact sink options.<br><br>Wall-hung units are supported by hangers or angle brackets. If you're installing a wall-hung sink for the first time, plan to add a support ledger. |

# BATHTUBS

Today's bathtub market overflows with styles. The 30 by 60-inch bathtub, which contributed to the predominance of the 5 by 7-foot bathroom, no longer rules. New and more comfortable tub shapes and sizes are available in an array of colors. Tubs can be purchased in whirlpool models and with grab bars and slip-resistant surfaces for safety. A white tub without special features is still the least expensive.

The boxy, familiar tub is enameled steel, relatively inexpensive, and lightweight. But it's also noisy, cold, and prone to chipping. Enameled cast-iron tubs are more durable and warmer to the touch, but they're very heavy. The most innovative tubs are vacuum-formed acrylic or injection-molded thermoplastic like ABS. These lightweight shells retain heat well, but their shiny surfaces can scratch or dull.

| Style | Characteristics |
| --- | --- |
| **Standard** 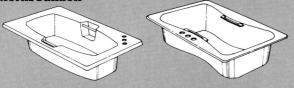 Recessed     Corner | Rectangular tubs come in two styles: recessed and corner. Recessed tubs fit between two side walls and against a back wall; they have one finished side. Corner models have one finished side and end and may be right or left-handed. If space allows, choose a longer model rather than the standard 60 inches; a depth of 16 inches or more is more comfortable than the standard 14 inches. |
| **Platform/sunken**   | Platform or sunken tubs, most commonly available in enameled cast iron or acrylic, are either set in a raised platform or sunk in the floor. Extra framing is often needed, especially for installation on an upper floor. Interior shapes and features vary. Built-in headrests, seating shelves, and grab bars abound. |
| **Freestanding** 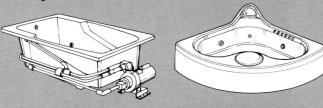 | An old-fashioned freestanding tub, such as the enduring clawfoot model, makes a nice focal point for a traditional design. You can buy reproductions or a reconditioned original. Such tubs can double as showers with the addition of Victorian-inspired shower head/diverter/curtain rod hardware. Recently, many new sources for renovators' supplies have sprung up; check specialty shops and antique plumbing catalogues. |
| **Whirlpool**  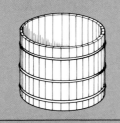 | Think of these hydromassage units simply as bathtubs with air jets. Jet designs vary; generally, you can opt for high volume and low pressure (a few strong jets) or low pressure and high volume (lots of softer jets). The best whirlpools are adjustable for water volume, air-water mixture, and direction. Because of their extra weight, whirlpools may need special floor framing. They may also require an extra-capacity water heater or separate in-line heater. |
| **Soaking** | Soaking tubs have deep interiors. Ideal for use in small spaces, they come in recessed, platform, and corner models, with rectangular or round interiors of fiberglass or acrylic. Hot tubs, with their continuous water supply, can present moisture problems in all but the best-ventilated spaces. They're best used outdoors. |

# SHOWERS

Many shower options are available, including shower and tub/shower kits that come with or without overlapping wall panels, adhesive, and caulking. You can also purchase shower and tub/shower wall kits to use with existing shower bases and tubs. If shower or tub/shower doors don't come with your kit, you can buy them separately. Because of their size, one-piece molded shower or tub/shower surrounds are used primarily in new homes or additions; if you have oversize doors in your house, you may be able to use one of these units.

Size is important; make sure you carefully measure the installation area and the unit before you buy. Units are available in fiberglass-reinforced plastic, acrylic, plastic laminate, and synthetic marble. Shower stalls made of tin or stainless steel are fading from the plumbing scene.

| Style | Characteristics |
|---|---|
| **Shower surrounds** 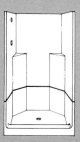 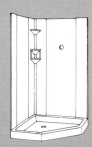 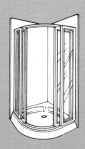 | Most shower surrounds require framing for support; you fasten the panel flanges to the framing. The shower base, walls, and door can be purchased individually or in a kit. Some models come with ceilings. For comfort, choose a shower that's at least 3 feet square. Complete assemblies vary in height, but 84 inches is common. Corner and circular shower models are available. Circular showers feature clear or tinted acrylic doors that double as walls. |
| **Tub/shower surrounds** 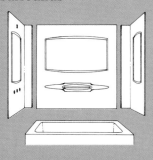 | Tub/shower surrounds must also have framing for support. You can purchase the tub, walls, and door in a kit, or buy a separate recessed tub and match it with compatible prefabricated wall panels or a custom wall treatment (such as tile panels). Molded fiberglass wall panels may include molded soap dishes, ledges, and grab bars. You can also add a shower head or install a hand-held shower attachment to convert an existing tub surround to a tub/shower. Shower attachments are mounted to the wall or tub spout. |
| **Shower bases**    Rectangular    Square    Corner | A shower base can be purchased separately or in a kit that includes a shower surround. Most bases are made of fiberglass, acrylic, or terrazzo, and come in standard sizes in rectangular, square, or corner shapes; all have a predrilled hole for the drain. It's easy to find a base that matches a tub or another fixture, as many manufacturers make both. |
| **Shower doors**   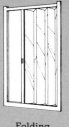 Swinging    Sliding    Folding | Doors for showers come in a variety of styles: swinging, sliding, and folding, as well as pivot (not shown). Tub/showers typically have sliding or folding doors. Doors and enclosures are commonly made of tempered safety glass with aluminum frames. Frames come in many finishes; you can select one to match your fittings. The glazing can be clear, hammered, pebbled, tinted, or striped. Many sliding doors have towel bars. Swinging, folding, and pivot doors can be installed with right or left openings. Folding doors are constructed of rigid plastic panels or flexible plastic sheeting. |

# FITTINGS FOR FIXTURES

Fittings are sold separately from fixtures. Select fittings that are durable and easy to use. Cost varies according to material, quality, and design.

Fittings for sinks are available with single, center-set, or spread-fit controls. A single-control fitting has a combined faucet and lever or knob that controls water flow and temperature. A center-set control has separate hot and cold water controls and a faucet, all mounted on a base. A spread-fit control has separate hot and cold water controls and a faucet, each independently mounted. The number of holes in the sink and the distances between them—either 4, 6, or 8 inches—determine which fittings can be used. If fittings

are to be attached to the wall or counter, the holes can be placed to suit the fittings.

For tubs and tub/showers, you can use either single or separate controls. Tubs also require a spout and drain. Tub/showers need a spout, shower head, diverter valve, and drain. Water-saver shower heads are readily available. You can purchase single-control fittings with pressure-balancing and temperature-limiting valves.

The best fittings are made of brass and come in several finishes, including chrome, pewter, gold, and bright enamel. Ceramic or nylon-disk designs are generally easier to maintain than older schemes.

## Styles

### Sink sets

| Single-control | Single-control with pull-out sprayer | Center-set | Spread-fit | Spread-fit |

### Shower sets

| Single-control | Temperature-limiting | Separate controls | Spray bars | Adjustable-height head |

### Tub sets

| Single-control | Separate controls | Separate controls | Deck-mount with separate controls | Roman spout with deck-mount controls |

### Tub/shower sets

| Single-control with diverter | Single-control with spout diverter | Separate controls with handle diverter | Separate controls with button diverter | Hand shower |

# TOILETS & BIDETS

New styling, new colors, and new technologies are updating the tried-and-true water closet. In addition to standard and antique models, toilets now come in sleek European designs, standard or low-profile heights, and rounded or elongated bowl shapes.

A washdown toilet, no longer accepted by many code authorities, is the least expensive, least efficient, and most noisy of the various models. Less noisy is a reverse trap toilet; it has a smaller water area, water seal, and trapway than the washdown.

A siphon jet toilet is quieter and has a larger water surface than the previous two styles, but it's also more costly; because it has a larger trapway, it's less likely to clog.

The new word in toilets is ultra-low-flush. Older toilets use 5 to 7 gallons of water or more per flush. In 1983, codes were changed to require 3½-gallon-per-flush toilets for new construction. But ultra-low-flush (ULF) toilets, which use only 1.6 gallons or less per flush, are already replacing these. Some homeowners complain that ULF toilets require several flushings. One solution to this problem is the pressure-assisted design, which uses a strong air vacuum to power a quick, intensive flush.

A bidet, best installed next to the toilet, is floor mounted and plumbed with hot and cold water. It's used primarily for personal hygiene.

Toilets and bidets are made of vitreous china.

| Style | Characteristics |
|---|---|
| **One-piece**  Low-profile    Wall-hung | One-piece toilets are characterized by their low profile, usually 19 to 26 inches high. These units are designed for floor and wall mounting. Available with round or elongated bowls, one-piece toilets have reverse trap, siphon jet, or ultra-low-flush flushing action. Their design, efficiency, and easy installation make them a popular choice. |
| **Two-piece**  Standard 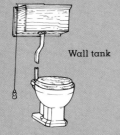 Wall tank  Safety  Ultra-low-flush | Two-piece toilets come in many models and can be mounted on the floor or on the wall. A wall-hung toilet, available only in siphon jet and siphon action models, offers easy access to the floor for cleaning. If you don't already have a wall-hung toilet, you'll face fairly major alterations to the wall framing and the floor.<br><br>If you have special needs, consider special toilet designs. The rim of a higher-seat safety toilet is 18 inches above the floor, compared to the 14-inch height of a conventional bowl. A back-outlet toilet has an above-floor drain. It's most frequently used on concrete floors, where it would be difficult and costly to install other toilets or relocate an existing one. |
| **Bidets**  Center-fit  Spread-fit | Available with wall or deck-mount water controls, a bidet comes with a spray spout or a vertical spray located in the center of the bowl. Some have rim jets for rinsing, to maintain bowl cleanliness. Most models also have a pop-up stopper that allows the unit to double as a foot bath or as a basin for washing clothes. |

# HEATING & VENTILATION

Nothing spoils the soothing effects of a long, hot soak or shower faster than stepping out into a cool bathroom. A small heater in the wall or ceiling may be just what you need to stay warm while toweling off.

Bathroom heaters warm rooms by two methods: convection (usually boosted by a small fan) and radiation. Convection heaters warm the air in a room; the air, in turn, transfers the heat to surfaces and objects that it contacts. Radiant heaters emit infrared or electromagnetic waves that warm the objects and surfaces they hit without warming the intervening air. If you're

installing a new slab or subfloor, you may want to consider radiant heating pipes below.

Most building codes require that bathrooms have either natural or forced ventilation. Forced ventilation, then, is required in windowless bathrooms. In fact, some codes specify that the exhaust fan must be on the same switch as the lights. But even if you have good natural ventilation, an exhaust fan can exchange the air in a bathroom faster than an open window; in bad weather, a fan can keep the elements out and still remove stale air.

| Style | Characteristics |
|---|---|
| **Electric heaters**   <br>Radiant heater with heat lamps    Convection heater with light and fan    Radiant or convection wall heater | Wall or ceiling-mounted convection heaters usually have an electrically heated resistance coil and a small fan to move the heated air. Radiant heaters using infrared light bulbs may be surface-mounted on the ceiling or recessed between joists. Radiant heating panels are generally flush-mounted on a wall or ceiling. |
| **Gas heaters**  <br>Convection wall heater    Freestanding heater | You'll find heaters available for either propane or natural gas. Though most are convection heaters, there is one radiant type: a catalytic heater. Most gas heaters are flush-mounted on a wall, but in a spacious master suite you might consider an attractive, freestanding "stove" unit. Options include electric ignition and wall-mounted thermostats. |
| **Heated towel bars** 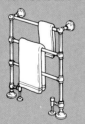 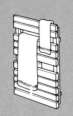<br>Hydronic towel bar    Electric towel bar | Besides gas and electricity, another heat source has reappeared on the bathroom scene: hot water. The original idea was to warm bath towels, but now these hydronic units—wall or floor-mounted—are being billed as radiators as well. You can find electric versions of the towel bar heater, too. |
| **Exhaust fans**   <br>Ceiling fan    Ceiling fan with light    Wall fan | You can buy fans to mount in the wall or ceiling. Some models are combined with a light or a heater, or both. The Home Ventilating Institute recommends that the fan be capable of exchanging the air at least eight times every hour (for details, see page 81). Most fans also have a noise rating measured in sones; the lower the number, the quieter the fan. |

# FLOORING

Think moisture-resistance when choosing a flooring material for a bathroom. Resilient tiles and sheets, ceramic tile, and properly sealed hardwood and stone are all good candidates. For a touch of comfort, don't rule out carpeting, especially the newer stain-resistant, industrial types.

For safety's sake, a bathroom floor must be slip-resistant, especially in wet areas. Tiles are safest in matte-finish versions. Smaller tiles, with their extra grout spaces, offer more traction than larger tiles. A rubberized mat or throw rug (if it will stay put) can provide firm footing near the tub or shower.

| Style | Characteristics |
|---|---|
| **Resilient** | Generally made of solid vinyl, rubber, or polyurethane, resilients are flexible, moisture and stain-resistant, easy to install, and simple to maintain. A seemingly endless variety of colors, textures, patterns, and styles is available. Resilient is vulnerable to dents and tears but can be repaired. Tiles can collect moisture between seams if improperly installed. Sheets run up to 12 feet wide, eliminating the need for seaming in many bathrooms; tiles are generally 12 inches square. Vinyl and rubber are comfortable to walk on. Polyurethane finish eliminates waxing. Vinyl is the least expensive option. Some vinyl comes with a photographically applied pattern, but most is inlaid; the latter style is more expensive but wears better. Tiles are often easier to lay than sheet goods. |
| **Ceramic tile** | Made of hard-fired slabs of clay, tiles are usually classified as *quarry* tile, commonly unglazed (unfinished) red-clay tiles that are rough and water-resistant; *pavers*, rugged unglazed tiles in earth-tone shades; and *glazed* tile, available in glossy, matte, or textured finishes and in many colors. Tile sizes run the gamut of widths, lengths, and thicknesses. Tile can be cold, noisy, and, if glazed, slippery underfoot. If not properly grouted, tiles can leak moisture. Grout spaces can be tough to keep clean. Cost varies widely; three-dimensional patterns and multicolored glazes can easily double costs. Purer clays fired at higher temperatures generally make costlier but better-wearing tiles. |
| **Wood** | Wood contributes warmth to the decor, feels good underfoot, resists wear, and can be refinished. The three basic types are *strip*, narrow tongue-and-groove boards in random lengths; *plank*, tongue-and-groove boards in various widths and random lengths; and wood *tile*, often laid in blocks or squares in parquet fashion. "Floating" floor systems have several veneered strips atop each tongue-and-groove backing board. Wood flooring may be factory-prefinished or unfinished. Moisture will damage wood flooring; also, an adequate floor substructure is crucial. Bleaching and some staining processes may wear unevenly and are difficult to repair. Wood is moderate to expensive in cost, depending on quality, finish, and installation. Floating systems are generally the most expensive. |
| **Stone** | Natural stone, such as slate, flagstone, marble, granite, and limestone, has been used for flooring for centuries. Today, its use is even more practical, thanks to the development of sealers and finishes. Easy to maintain, stone flooring is also virtually indestructible. Stone can be used in its natural shape or cut into uniform pieces—rectangular blocks or more formal tiles. Generally, uniform pieces are butted tightly together; irregular flagstone requires grouted joints. The cost of most stone flooring is high. Moreover, the weight of the materials requires a very strong, well-supported subfloor. Some stone—marble in particular—is cold and slippery underfoot. Careful sealing is a must; some stones absorb stains and dirt readily. |

# WALL COVERINGS

In addition to the shower and tub-surround areas, your bathroom will probably include a good bit of wall space. Bathroom wall treatments must be able to withstand moisture, heat, and high usage. These surfaces also go a long way toward defining the overall impact of your bath. (For details on paint, see page 101.)

| Style | Characteristics |
| --- | --- |
| **Ceramic tiles** | Wall tiles are glazed and offer great variety in color and design. Generally lighter and thinner than floor tiles, they're used primarily on interior surfaces—walls, countertops, and ceilings. Their relatively light weight is a plus for vertical installation. The glazed surface is water-resistant, though the bodies are porous.<br><br>Standard sizes for wall tiles range from 3-inch squares to 4¼ by 8½-inch rectangles; thicknesses vary from ¼ to ⅜ inch. Other sizes and shapes are available. Many wall tiles come with matching trim pieces for edges, coves, and corners.<br><br>Wall tiles are also available in pregrouted panels, a handy shortcut that reduces installation time and effort. Designed primarily for tub and shower areas, a panel contains up to 64 tiles, each measuring 4¼ inches square. The panels have flexible, water-repellent grout.<br><br>Ceramic mosaic is one of the most colorful and versatile materials in the tile family. Tiles sold under this name are generally small—2 by 2 inches or less. For this reason, they can be installed on curved surfaces. Mosaics come in sheets, with the tiles mounted on thread mesh or paper backing or joined with silicone rubber. Once they're in place, you grout these sheets like any other wall tiles. |
| **Stone** | Marble, slate, limestone, and granite, whether as 8 or 12-inch tiles or wider sheets, can perform a role similar to ceramic tile. Stone tiles are expensive but, used as accents, they can go a long way. Most stone, especially marble, should be thoroughly sealed for wall use; untreated, it can be stained or eaten away by acids in cleaning supplies or even household water. |
| **Glass block** | If you're looking for some ambient daylight but don't want to sacrifice privacy, consider glass blocks. You can buy 3 or 4-inch-thick square blocks in many sizes; rectangular blocks are available in a more limited selection. Textures can be smooth, wavy, rippled, bubbly, or crosshatched. Mortarless block systems make an often tricky installation job simpler for do-it-yourselfers. |
| **Wallpaper** | Wallpaper for the bathroom should be scrubbable, durable, and stain-resistant. Solid-vinyl wallpapers, which come in a wide variety of colors and textures, fit the bill. New patterns, including some that replicate other surfaces (such as linen), are generally subtle; wallpaper borders add visual punch to ceiling lines and openings. Good ventilation is crucial to keep wallpaper from loosening. |
| **Plaster** | The textured, uneven, and slightly rounded edges of plaster give a bathroom a custom, informal look. Plaster is especially popular for Southwest-theme designs. If the surface is too irregular, however, plaster is hard to keep clean. |
| **Wood** | Tongue-and-groove wood paneling—natural, stained, bleached, or painted—provides a charming accent to country schemes. Wainscoting is the most popular application; the paneling is separated from wallpaper or paint above by the traditional chair rail.<br><br>Moldings are back in vogue. Specialty shops are likely to have a wide selection and will often custom-match an old favorite to order. |

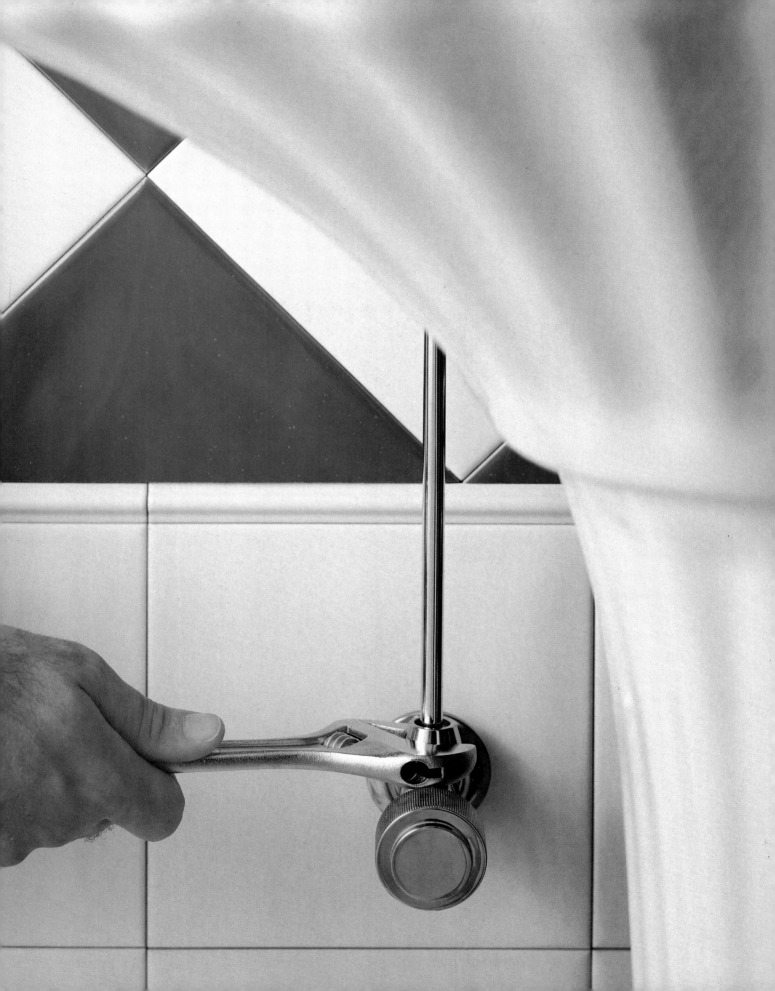

# REMODELING BASICS

## Installation ▪ Removal ▪ Tools ▪ Techniques

**A**fter sifting through a wealth of bathroom remodeling ideas, you've probably selected what's right for your family's special needs. Perhaps you've decided on a quick and easy change—a fresh coat of paint in your favorite color. Or maybe this is the time for the major remodel you've been dreaming about—moving a wall, opening the ceiling with a skylight, installing a gleaming new tub and surrounding tile.

This chapter is designed to help you translate your ideas and dreams into changes in your bathroom. From the basics of structural framing, plumbing, and wiring to the fine points of installing the walls, it's all here for you to read and do. Each project begins with general information on planning and procedures, then takes you through the work with illustrated step-by-step instructions.

Though the directions assume that you have some basic knowledge of building terms, tools, materials, and techniques, you needn't be an expert to do most of the projects in this chapter. If you need more detailed information on procedures, take a look at the Southern Living books *Basic Carpentry, Basic Plumbing,* and *Basic Home Wiring.*

**Pedestal sinks** are making a comeback, and most models are easy to install. Since plumbing hardware will be visible below the sink, you may wish to invest in decorative supply tubing and shutoff valves. For installation details, see pages 84–85.

# Before work begins

Are you ready to remodel? Before plunging into a project, you should have a clear idea of the steps required to complete the job, and the sequence in which they should be done. You'll also need to evaluate your own ability to perform the various tasks. One of your first decisions will be whether to do the work yourself or get professional help.

## Can you do the work yourself?

What skills do you need to remodel a bathroom? It depends on the improvements you're planning. Projects such as painting, setting wall tile, and installing floors and cabinets are within easy reach of any homeowner with basic do-it-yourself ability. You'll need a few specialized tools to complete some projects, but you can buy them at a building supply or home improvement center, or perhaps even rent them.

If your plans include complex remodeling projects such as moving bearing walls, running new drain and vent pipes, or wiring new electrical circuits and service panels, you may want to hire professionals to do part or all of the job. But many smaller structural, plumbing, and electrical jobs can be done by a homeowner with some basic experience.

Even if there's little you can build, you may discover a talent for demolition—and save some money. But some contractors may not want to relinquish this task. If you do take it on, be sure to finish by the time the remodeling crew is ready to begin.

## Planning your project

Putting careful thought into your preparations can save you extra work and inconvenience later. As the scale of your remodeling project increases, the need for careful planning becomes more critical. If your home has only one bathroom, your goal is to keep it in operating order as much of the time as possible. With careful scheduling, the remodeling time will be easier for the entire family.

Be sure to obtain any necessary permits from your local building department. A contractor, if you hire one, will do this job for you. But if you're doing the work yourself, you'll need to secure permits and arrange for inspections. Finally, before you start work, double-check the priorities listed below.

■ Establish the sequence of jobs to be done, and estimate the time needed for completion.

■ If you're hiring professional help, make sure you have legally binding contracts and schedules with contractors and subcontractors.

■ If electricity, gas, or water must be shut off by the utility company, arrange for the cutoff date.

■ Locate an area for temporarily storing fixtures that have been removed.

■ Measure fixtures for adequate clearance through doorways and hallways, or down staircases.

■ Locate a site for dumping refuse and secure necessary permits.

■ Obtain all other required permits.

■ Arrange for timely delivery of materials and be sure you have all the necessary tools on hand.

Note: If you're contracting the work, you can skip the last three steps; they're normally part of the contractor's service.

## How to use this chapter

Reading all the sections of this chapter through quickly will help you to get a general feeling for what's involved in bathroom remodeling.

In the first three sections, you'll find an overview of structural, plumbing, and electrical systems. Even if you don't plan to do the work yourself, you may want to review these sections for background information. Understanding basic systems enables you to plan more effectively and to understand the reasons for code restrictions affecting your plans.

Many of your remodeling hours may be spent tearing out old work. To minimize the effort, we've included removal procedures along with installation instructions in the sections on fixtures, wall coverings, flooring, and cabinets.

If you're planning only one or two small projects, turn directly to the applicable sections for step-by-step instructions.

## STEPS IN REMODELING

You can use this chart to plan the general order of removal and installation in remodeling your bathroom, though you may need to alter the suggested order, depending on the scale of your job and the materials you select. For more information, read the appropriate sections on the following pages. Manufacturers' instructions will offer additional guidelines as you go along.

### Removal sequence

1. Accessories, decorative elements
2. Furniture, if any
3. Contents of cabinets, closets, shelves
4. Fixtures, plumbing fittings
5. Vanity countertops
6. Vanity cabinets, recessed cabinets, shelves
7. Flooring
8. Light fixtures, as required
9. Wall and ceiling coverings

### Installation sequence

1. Structural changes: walls, doors, windows, skylights
2. Rough plumbing changes
3. Electrical wiring
4. Bathtub, shower
5. Wall and ceiling coverings
6. Light fixtures
7. Vanity cabinets, countertops
8. Toilets, bidets, sinks
9. Wall cabinets, shelves
10. Flooring
11. Accessories, decorative elements

# Structural basics

Understanding your home's structural shell is a good way to begin any home improvement project, including bathroom remodeling.

Your house's framework probably will conform to the pattern of the "typical house" shown in the illustration below. Starting at the base of the drawing, you'll notice the following framing members: a wooden sill resting on a foundation wall; a series of horizontal, evenly spaced floor joists; and a subfloor (usually plywood sheets) laid atop the joists. This platform supports the first-floor walls, both interior and exterior. The walls are formed by vertical, evenly spaced studs that run between a horizontal sole plate and parallel top plate. The primary wall coverings are fastened directly to the studs.

Depending on the design of the house, one of several types of construction may be used above the first-floor walls. If there's a second story, a layer of ceiling joists rests on the walls; these joists support both the floor above and the ceiling below. A one-story house will have either an "open-beamed" ceiling—flat or pitched—or a "finished" ceiling. With a flat roof, the finished ceiling is attached directly to the rafters. The ceiling below a pitched roof is attached to joists.

## Removing a partition wall

Sometimes major bathroom remodeling entails removing all or part of an interior wall to enlarge the space.

Walls that define your bathroom may be bearing or nonbearing. A bearing wall helps support the weight of the house; a nonbearing wall does not. An interior nonbearing wall, often called a partition wall, may be removed without special precautions. The procedure outlined in this section applies to partitions only. If you're considering a remodeling project that involves moving a bearing wall, consult an architect or contractor about problems and procedures.

How can you tell the difference in walls? All exterior walls running perpendicular to ceiling and floor joists are bearing. At least one main interior wall may be a bearing wall.

To determine whether the wall you're planning to move is bearing, climb up into the attic or crawlspace and check the ceiling joists. If they are joined over any wall, that wall is bearing. Even if joists span the entire width of the house, their midsections may be supported by a bearing wall at the point of maximum allowable span. If you have any doubts about the wall, consult an architect, contractor, or building inspector.

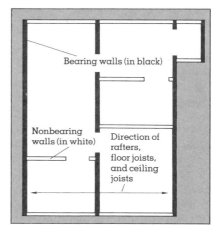

Bearing walls (in black)

Nonbearing walls (in white)

Direction of rafters, floor joists, and ceiling joists

Though removing a partition wall is not complicated, it can be quite messy. Cover the floors and fixtures, and wear a dust mask, safety glasses, and gloves. NOTE: Check the wall for signs of wiring, supply and drain pipes, and heating and ventilation ducts; you'll have to reroute them.

**Remove the wall covering.** First, if there's a door in the wall, remove it from its hinges. Pry off any door trim, ceiling molding, and base molding.

The most common wall covering is gypsum wallboard nailed to wall studs. To remove it, use a prybar (see "Removing gypsum wallboard," page 98).

If the wall covering is plaster and lath, chisel away the plaster and cut the lath backing—wood strips or metal—so that you can pry off the pieces of lath and plaster.

*(Continued on next page)*

## TYPICAL HOUSE STRUCTURE

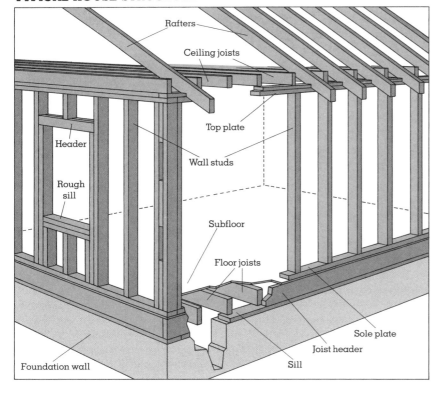

Rafters

Ceiling joists

Top plate

Header

Wall studs

Rough sill

Subfloor

Floor joists

Sole plate

Joist header

Sill

Foundation wall

■ **Structural basics**

### DISMANTLING THE WALL FRAMING

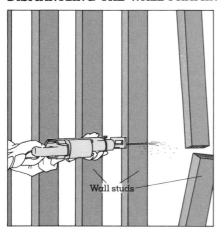

**Saw through the middle** of the wall studs; bend the studs sideways to free the nails from the top and sole plates.

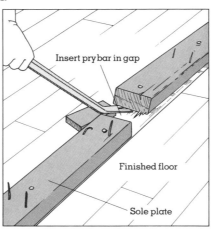

**Cut gaps** through the sole plate with a saw and chisel; insert a prybar in each gap and lift to free the sole plate.

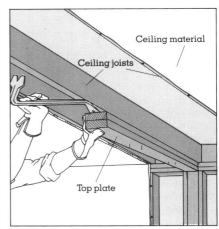

**Strip ceiling materials** back from the top plate, cut gaps in the plate, and pry out sections of plate.

**Dismantle the framing.** Remove studs by sawing through the middle of each one; then push and pull them sideways to free the nails (see illustration above).

To remove the sole plate, saw a small section out of the middle down to the finished floor level, chisel through the remaining thickness, and insert a prybar in the gap.

To remove a top plate that lies parallel to the joists, cut ceiling materials back to adjacent joists, and pry off the plate. If the top plate is perpendicular to the joists, you are probably working on a bearing wall and will have to take special precautions (see page 67).

**Patch walls, ceiling, and floor.** Holes in wallboard and plaster aren't difficult to patch; the real challenge lies in matching a special texture, wallpaper, shade of paint, or well-aged floor. This is not a problem if your remodeling plans call for new wall coverings, ceiling, or flooring. In either case, see the sections "Walls & ceilings" (pages 98–105) and "Flooring" (pages 106–108) for techniques and tips.

### Framing a new wall

To subdivide a large bathroom or to enlarge a cramped one, you may need to build a new partition wall or partial wall. Components of wall framing are illustrated below.

Framing a wall is a straightforward task, but you must measure carefully and check the alignment as work progresses. The basic steps are listed below. If you plan to install a doorway, see pages 69–70.

**Plot the location.** The new wall must be anchored securely to existing ceiling joists, the floor, and, at least on one side, to wall studs. To locate the studs, try knocking with your fist along the wall until the sound changes from hollow to solid.

If you have wallboard, you can use an inexpensive stud finder; often, though, the nails that hold wallboard to the studs are visible on close inspection.

To locate ceiling joists, use the same methods or, from the attic or crawlspace, drill small holes down through the ceiling on both sides of a joist to serve as reference points below. Adjacent joists and studs should be evenly spaced, usually about 16 or 24 inches apart.

### WALL FRAMING COMPONENTS

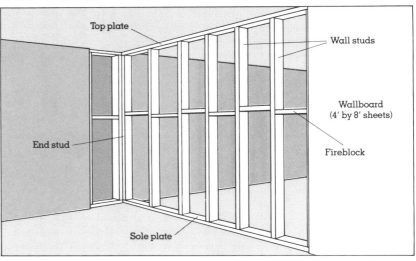

A wall running perpendicular to the joists will demand the least effort to attach. If wall and joists will run parallel, though, try to center the wall under a single joist; otherwise, you'll need to remove ceiling materials between two parallel joists and install nailing blocks every 2 feet (see illustrations at right). If the side of the new wall falls between existing studs, you'll need to install additional nailing blocks.

On the ceiling, mark both ends of the center line of the new wall. Measure 1¾ inches (half the width of the top plate) on both sides of each mark. Snap parallel lines between corresponding marks with a chalk line; the top plate will occupy the space between the lines.

**Position the sole plate.** Hang a plumb bob from each end of the lines you just marked and mark these new points on the floor. Snap two more chalk lines to connect these points.

Cut both sole plate and top plate to the desired length. Lay the sole plate between the lines on the floor and nail it in place with 10-penny nails spaced every 2 feet. (If you have a masonry floor, use a masonry bit to drill a bolt hole through the sole plate every 2 or 3 feet. Insert expansion anchors for lag bolts and bolt the sole plate to the floor.)

If you're planning a doorway (see "Framing a doorway," below), don't nail through that section of the plate; it will be cut out later.

**Mark stud positions.** Lay the top plate against the sole plate, as shown in the illustration. Beginning

### ANCHORING A TOP PLATE

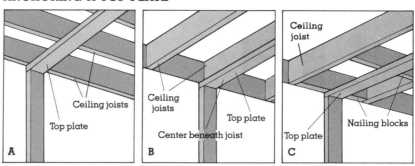

To anchor a top plate, nail to perpendicular joists (A) or to the bottom of the parallel joist (B), or install nailing blocks between parallel joists (C).

at the end that will be attached to an existing stud or to nailing blocks, measure in 1½ inches—the thickness of a 2 by 4 stud—and draw a line across both plates with a combination square. Starting once more from that end, measure and draw lines at 15¼ and 16¾ inches. From these lines, advance 16 inches. Don't worry if the spacing at the far end is less than 16 inches. (If local codes permit, consider a 24-inch spacing—you'll save lumber—and adjust the placement of lines to 23¼ and 24¾ inches.)

**Fasten the top plate.** While two helpers hold the top plate in position between the lines (marked on the ceiling), nail it to perpendicular joists, to one parallel joist, or to nailing blocks, as shown above.

**Attach the studs.** Measure and cut the studs to exact length. Attach one end stud (or both) to existing studs or to nailing blocks between studs. Lift

the remaining studs into place one at a time; line them up on the marks, and check plumb with a carpenter's level. Toenail the studs to both top plate and sole plate with 8-penny nails.

Many building codes require horizontal fireblocks between studs. The number of rows depends on the code; if permitted, position blocks to provide an extra nailing surface for wall materials.

**Finish.** After the studs are installed, it's time to add any electrical outlets and switches (see pages 76–78), as well as any new plumbing (see pages 72–75). It's also time for the building inspector to check your work. Following the inspection, you can finish the walls (see pages 98–105).

### Framing a doorway

Your remodeling may call for changing the position of a door and creating a new door opening. Be sure the wall you plan to cut into is a nonbearing wall (see page 67); if it's a bearing wall, consult a professional.

**Position the opening.** This section assumes that you're installing a standard prehung door and frame. Before starting work, check the manufacturer's "rough opening" dimensions—the exact wall opening required after the new framing is in place.

You'll need to plan an opening large enough to accommodate both

### MARKING STUD POSITIONS

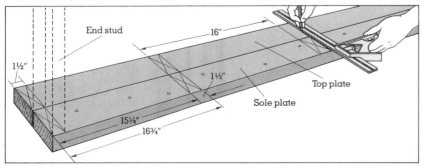

## ■ Structural basics

the rough opening and the rough door framing—an additional 1½ inches on top and sides. If your door didn't come with rough opening dimensions, add an additional ⅜ inch all around for shimming (adjusting level and plumb) the typical door frame.

Often it's simpler to remove the wallboard from floor to ceiling between two bordering studs (the new king studs) that will remain in place. (This is the method illustrated.) In any case, you'll save work later if you can use at least one existing stud as part of the new framing.

Regardless of the method you choose, use a carpenter's level for a straightedge, and mark the outline of the opening on the wall.

**Remove wall covering and studs.** First remove any base molding. Cut along the outline of the opening with a reciprocating or keyhole saw, being careful to cut only the wallboard, not the studs beneath. Pry the wallboard away from the framing. To remove plaster and lath, chisel through the plaster to expose the lath; then cut the lath, and pry lath and plaster loose.

Cut the studs inside the opening to the height required for the header (see illustration below). Using a combination square, mark these studs on the face and one side, then

cut carefully with a reciprocating or crosscut saw. Remove the cut studs from the sole plate.

**Frame the opening.** With wall covering and studs removed, you're ready to frame the opening. Measure and cut the header (for a partition wall you can use a 2 by 4 laid flat), and toenail it to the king studs with 8-penny nails. Nail the header to the bottoms of the cripple studs.

Cut the part of the sole plate within the opening, and pry it away from the subfloor (see "Removing a partition wall," page 67).

Cut trimmer studs and nail them to the king studs with 10-penny nails in a staggered pattern. You'll probably need to adjust the width by blocking out a third trimmer from one side, as shown below right. Leave an extra ⅜ inch on each side for shimming, plus space for the door jambs.

**Hang the door.** A standard prehung door and frame are predrilled for a lockset. The door comes already fitted and attached to the frame with hinges. Pull out the hinge pins to remove the door before you install the frame. Nail the frame in the rough opening, shimming carefully to make the side jambs plumb and the head jamb level. Rehang the

door and install the lockset; then install stop molding and trim (casing).

### Closing a doorway

It's easy to eliminate an existing doorway. Simply add new studs within the opening and attach new wall coverings. The only trick is to match the present wall surface.

First, remove the casing around the opening. Then remove the door from its hinges or guide track, and pry any jambs or tracks away from the rough framing.

Next, measure the gap on the floor between the existing trimmer studs; cut a length of 2 by 4 to serve as a new sole plate. Nail it to the floor with 10-penny nails. (If you have a masonry floor, attach the 2 by 4 with lag bolts and expansion anchors).

Measure and cut new studs to fill the space; position one stud beneath each cripple stud. Toenail the studs to the new sole plate and header with 8-penny nails. Add fireblocks between studs if required by the local code.

Strip the wall coverings back far enough to give yourself a firm nailing surface and an even edge. Then add new coverings to match the existing ones, or resurface the entire wall (see pages 98–105). Match or replace the baseboard molding.

### FRAMING A DOORWAY

**Mark and cut studs** within the opening to a height even with the top of the new header, and remove.

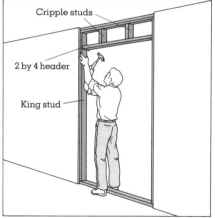

**Nail the new header** to the king studs, then nail through the header into the ends of the new cripple studs.

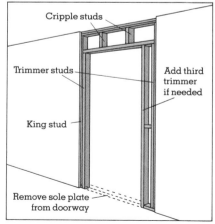

**Nail trimmer studs** to the king studs; add a third trimmer, if needed, to make the opening the correct width.

# SKYLIGHTING THE BATHROOM

A skylight brings light and an open feeling into windowless interior bathrooms or those where uncovered windows would be a privacy problem.

Installing a skylight in a pitched roof with asphalt or wood shingles is a two-part process: you cut and frame openings in both roof and ceiling, and connect the two openings with a vertical light shaft. (You don't even need a light shaft for a flat roof or open-beamed ceiling.) A description of the installation sequence follows; for more detailed information, consult the manufacturer's instructions or your skylight dealer.

**Mark the openings.** Begin by measuring and marking the location of the ceiling opening. Then drive nails up through the four corners and center so they'll be visible in the attic. You'll save work if you can use one or two ceiling joists as the edges of your opening.

With a plumb bob, transfer the center mark to the underside of the roof. Mark the roof opening suggested by the manufacturer on the underside of the roof and drive nails through the corners.

**Frame the roof opening.** Exercise extreme caution when working on the roof; if the pitch is steep or if you have a tile or slate roof, you should leave this part to professionals.

If your skylight must be mounted on a curb frame, build the curb first; 2 by 6 lumber is commonly used.

To determine the actual size of the opening you need to cut, add the dimensions of any framing materials to the rough opening size marked by the nails. You may need to remove some extra shingles or roofing materials down to the sheathing to accommodate the flashing of a curb-mount-

**BASIC PARTS OF A SKYLIGHT**

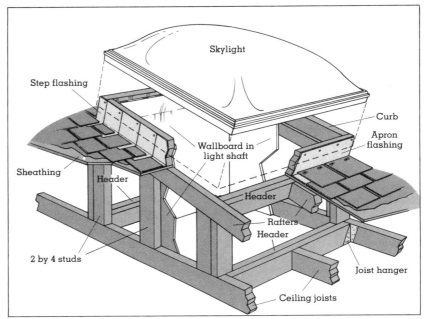

ed skylight or the flange of a self-flashing unit.

Cut the roof opening in successive layers: roofing materials first, sheathing next, and finally the rafters. Before cutting the rafters, support them with 2 by 4s nailed to the ceiling joists below.

To frame the opening, you'll need double headers and possibly trimmers to narrow the width between rafters.

If you're installing a curb-mounted unit, position and flash the curb. Toenail the curb to the rafters or trimmers and to the headers. Flash according to the manufacturer's instructions.

**Mount the skylight.** For a curb-mounted unit, secure the skylight to the top of the curb with nails and a sealant. Nail a self-flashing unit

through the flange directly to the roof sheathing; then coat the joints and nail holes with roofing cement.

**Open the ceiling.** Cut through the ceiling materials and then cut the joists. Support joists to be cut by bracing them against adjacent joists. Frame the opening in the manner used for the roof opening.

**Build a light shaft.** Measure the distance between the ceiling headers and roof headers at each corner and at 16-inch intervals between the corners. Cut studs to fit the measurements and install them as illustrated above. This provides a nailing surface for wall coverings.

To finish, insulate the spaces between studs in the light shaft before fastening wall coverings to the studs. Trim the ceiling opening with molding strips.

# Plumbing basics

Whether you're planning to add a single fixture or remodel an entire bathroom, you'll need an introduction to plumbing basics. Replacing an old bathtub, sink, or toilet with a new one at the same location is a straightforward job, but roughing-in (installing) plumbing for fixtures at new locations takes skill and planning.

What follows is an overview of fundamentals—household plumbing systems, plumbing codes, and general procedures for planning, routing, and roughing-in new pipes. This information may help you to decide whether to make your project a do-it-yourself effort or a professional one. If you have doubts, consider a compromise—you might hire a professional to check your plans and install pipes, then make the fixture hookups yourself (see pages 82–97).

If you want to do all the work yourself, read the information that follows before you begin to ensure that you're familiar with the tools and techniques required for the job.

## How the system works

Three complementary sets of pipes work together to fill your home's plumbing needs: the water supply system, and the drain-waste and vent (DWV) systems (see the illustration below).

**The supply system.** Water for your toilet, tub, shower, and sink enters the house from a public water main or from a source on the property. Water from a water company is usually delivered through a water meter and a main shutoff valve. You'll find the meter either in your basement or crawlspace, or outdoors, near your property line. The main shutoff valve—which turns the water for the whole house on and off—is usually situated near the water meter.

At the water service entrance, the main supply line divides in two—one line branching off to be heated by the water heater, the other remaining as cold water. The two pipes usually run parallel below the first-floor level until they reach the vicinity of a group of fixtures, then

head up through the wall or floor. Sometimes the water supply—hot, cold, or both—passes through a water softener or filter before reaching the fixtures.

Supply pipes are installed with a slight pitch in the runs, sloping back toward the lowest point in the system so that all pipes can be drained. Sometimes at the lowest point there's a valve that can be opened to drain the system—essential for vacation homes in cold climates.

**Drain-waste and vent systems.** The drain-waste pipes take advantage of gravity to channel waste water and solid wastes to the house sewer line. Vent pipes carry away sewer gas and maintain atmospheric pressure in drainpipes and fixture traps. The traps (curved sections in the fixtures' drainpipes) remain filled with water at all times to keep gases from coming up the drains.

Every house has a 3 or 4-inch-diameter main soil stack that serves a dual function. Below the level of the fixtures, it is your home's primary drainpipe; above the stack it becomes a vent with its upper end protruding through the roof. Drainpipes from individual fixtures, as well as branch drains, connect to the main stack. These pipes lead away from all fixtures at a carefully calculated slope—normally ¼ inch per foot. Since any system may clog now and then, cleanouts usually are placed at the upper end of each horizontal section of drainpipe.

A fixture or fixture group located on a branch drain far from the main stack will have a secondary vent stack of its own rising to the roof.

## Planning and layout

This section outlines the planning process and explores some of your options in adding new plumbing. When plotting out any plumbing addition you must balance code restrictions, the limitations of your system's layout, design considerations, and, of course, your own plumbing abilities.

## A PLUMBING OVERVIEW

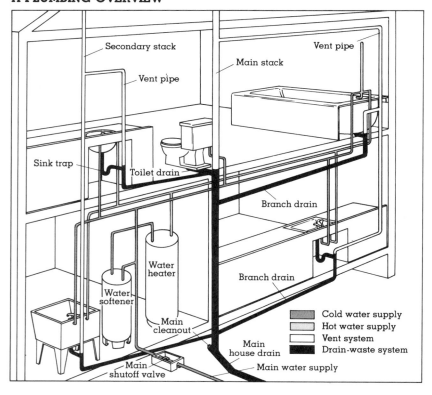

Secondary stack
Vent pipe
Vent pipe
Main stack
Sink trap
Toilet drain
Branch drain
Water heater
Water softener
Branch drain
Main cleanout
Main house drain
Main water supply
Main shutoff valve

Cold water supply
Hot water supply
Vent system
Drain-waste system

**Check the codes.** Almost any improvement that adds pipe to the system will require approval from local building department officials before you start, and inspection of the work before you close the walls and floor.

Learn what work you may do yourself—some codes require that certain work be done only by licensed plumbers.

**Map your system.** A detailed map of your present system will give you a clear picture of where it's feasible to tie into supply and drain lines, and whether the present drains and vents are adequate for the use you plan.

Starting in the basement, sketch in the main soil stack, branch drains, house drain, and accessible cleanouts; then trace the networks of hot and cold supply pipes. Also, check the attic or roof for the course of the main stack and any secondary vent stacks. Determine and mark on the sketch the materials and, if possible, the diameters of all pipes (see "Materials," at right).

**Layout options.** Plan the plumbing for any new fixtures in three parts: supply, drainage, and venting. To minimize cost and keep the work simple, arrange a fixture or group of fixtures so they are as close to the present pipes as possible.

Three economical ways to group your new fixtures (see drawings below) are to:

■ connect an individual fixture to the existing stack (drawing A)

■ add a fixture or group above or below an existing group on the stack

■ tie a fixture (except a toilet) directly into a new or existing branch drain (drawing B)

If your addition is planned for an area across the house from the existing plumbing, you'll probably need to run a new secondary vent stack up through the roof, and a new branch drain to the soil stack (see drawing B below) or to the main house drain via an existing cleanout.

The new vent stack must be installed inside an existing wall (a big job), built into a new oversize or "thickened" wall (see "Build a wet wall," page 74), or concealed in a closet or cabinet. In mild climates, a vent may also run up the exterior of the house, but it must be hidden within a box.

**Materials.** Decide what kind of pipe you'll need, based on the material of the pipe you'll be tying into.

Your home's supply pipes most likely are either galvanized steel (referred to as "galvanized" or "iron"

pipe) connected by threaded fittings, or rigid copper joined with soldered fittings.

Older DWV pipes probably are made of cast iron, with "hub" or "bell-and-spigot" ends joined by molten lead and oakum. (DWV pipes other than the main stack may be galvanized.)

To extend cast-iron pipes, you may substitute "hubless" fittings (consisting of neoprene gaskets and stainless steel clamps), which are simpler to install than hub fittings.

If you wish to change pipe material in your extension, it's a matter of inserting the appropriate adapter at the fitting end. You might want to change cast-iron or galvanized pipe to copper or plastic pipe. First check your local code, because some areas prohibit use of plastic pipe.

## Plumbing codes

Few code restrictions apply to simple extensions of hot and cold water supply pipes, provided your house's water pressure is up to the task. The material and diameter for supply pipes serving each new fixture or appliance are spelled out clearly in the plumbing code. More troublesome are the pipes that make up the DWV system. Codes are quite specific about the following: the size of stacks, drainpipes, and vents serving any new fixture requiring drainage; the critical distance from fixture traps to the stack; and the method of venting fixtures.

**Stack, drain, and vent size.** The plumbing code will specify minimum diameters for stacks and vents in relation to numbers of *fixture units.* (One fixture unit represents 7.5 gallons or 1 cubic foot of water per minute.) In the code you'll find fixture unit ratings for all plumbing fixtures given in chart form.

To determine drainpipe diameter, look up the fixture or fixtures you're considering on the code's fixture unit chart. Add up the total fixture units; then look up the drain diameter specified for that number of units.

## PLUMBING LAYOUT OPTIONS

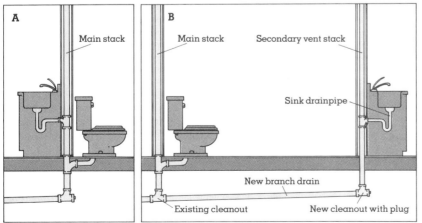

**To drain bathroom plumbing additions,** you can either (A) tap into the present main stack, if nearby, or (B) install a new branch drain and secondary vent stack.

*(Continued on next page)*

# ■Plumbing basics

Vent pipe sizing criteria also include *length* of vent and *type* of vent, in addition to fixture unit load.

**Critical distance.** The maximum distance allowed between a fixture's trap and the stack or main drain that it empties into is called the critical distance. No drain outlet may be completely below the level of the trap's crown weir (see illustration below)—if it were, it would act as a siphon, draining the trap. Thus, when the ideal drainpipe slope of ¼ inch per foot is figured in, the length of that drainpipe quickly becomes limited. But if the fixture drain is *vented* properly within the critical distance, the drainpipe may run on indefinitely to the actual stack or main drain.

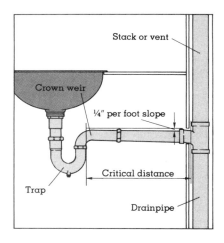

**Venting options.** The four basic venting options (see illustration above right)—subject to local code—are wet venting, back venting, individual venting, and indirect venting.

■ *Wet venting* is simplest—the fixture is vented directly through the fixture drain to the soil stack.

■ *Back venting (reventing)* involves running a vent loop up past fixtures to reconnect with the main stack or secondary vent above the fixture level.

■ *Individual (secondary) venting* means running a secondary vent stack up through the roof for a new fixture or group of fixtures distant from the main stack.

## VENTING OPTIONS

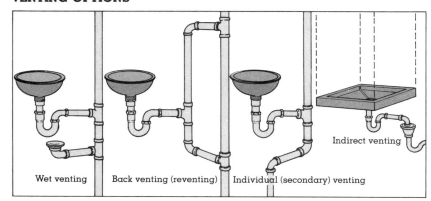

Wet venting    Back venting (reventing)    Individual (secondary) venting    Indirect venting

■ *Indirect venting* allows you to vent some fixtures (such as a basement shower) into an existing floor drain or laundry tub without further venting.

## Roughing-in new plumbing

Once you've planned your plumbing additions, you can begin installation.

**Locate and tie into existing pipe.** In the mapping stage, you determined the rough locations of the pipes. The next step is to pinpoint them and cut away wall, ceiling, or floor coverings along studs or joists to expose the sections you want to tie into. Be sure to cut out holes large enough to allow you to work comfortably. (For information about wall and floor coverings, see pages 98–108.)

Basically, tying into drainwaste, vent, and supply lines entails cutting a section out of each pipe and inserting a new fitting to join old and new pipe. The method you use to tie into the pipes varies with the pipe material.

**Route new pipes.** With the connections made, the new DWV and supply pipes are run to the new fixture location. Ideally, new drainpipes should be routed below the bathroom floor. They can be suspended from floor joists by pipe hangers, inserted in the space between parallel joists, or run through

notches or holes drilled in joists that are at right angles to the pipe (if allowed by code). If you have a finished basement or your bathroom is on the second floor, you'll need to cut into the floor or ceiling to install pipes between or through joists, hide the pipes with a dropped ceiling, or box them in. (Remember that drainpipes must slope away from fixtures at a minimum slope of ¼ inch per foot.)

Supply pipes normally follow drainpipes but can be routed directly up through the wall or floor from main horizontal lines. Supply pipes should run parallel, at least 6 inches apart. In cold areas, codes may prohibit supply pipes in exterior walls.

**Build a wet wall.** The main soil stack, and often a secondary stack, commonly hide inside an oversize house wall called a "wet wall."

Unlike an ordinary 2 by 4 stud wall (shown on page 68), a wet wall has a sole plate and a top plate built from 2 by 6 or 2 by 8 lumber. Additionally, the 2 by 4 studs are set in pairs, with flat sides facing out. This creates maximum space inside the wall for large DWV pipes (which often have an outer diameter greater than 3½ inches) and for fittings, which are wider yet.

You can also "fur out" an existing wall to hide added pipes—attach new 2 by 4s to the old ones, then add new wall coverings. Similarly, a new branch drain that can't run below the floor may be hidden by a raised section of floor.

## Roughing-in fixtures

Following are general notes on roughing-in new fixtures that require tying into your present DWV and supply systems, or extending them. Note that fixtures may be required to have air chambers—dead-end pipes that minimize noisy water hammer.

**Sink.** A sink is comparatively easy to install. Common installations are back-to-back (requires little pipe), within a vanity cabinet (hides pipe runs), and side-by-side. A sink can often be wet vented if it's within the critical distance; otherwise it's back vented. Adding a sink has little impact on the drain's present efficiency (a sink rates low in fixture units).

Supply pipes required: Hot and cold stubouts with shutoff valves; transition fittings, if necessary; flexible tubing above shutoff valves (see "Sink faucets," page 92).

**Toilet.** The single most troublesome fixture to install, a toilet requires its own vent (2-inch minimum) and at least a 3-inch drain. If it's on a branch drain, a toilet can't be upstream from a sink or shower.

The closet bend and toilet floor flange must be roughed-in first; the floor flange must be positioned at the level of the eventual finished floor.

Supply pipes required: Cold water stubout with shutoff valve; flexible tubing above valve (see "Installing a toilet," page 96).

**Shower stall and bathtub.** Like sinks, bathtubs and showers rate low in fixture units. They're often positioned on branch drains and are usually wet-vented or back-vented; both enter the stack at floor level or below because of the below-floor trap. A shower's faucet body and shower head assembly are installed while the wall is open; tubs and showers may require support framing.

Supply pipes required: Hot and cold supply lines and a pipe to the shower head (see "Bathtub & shower faucets," page 93).

## ROUGHING-IN FIXTURES

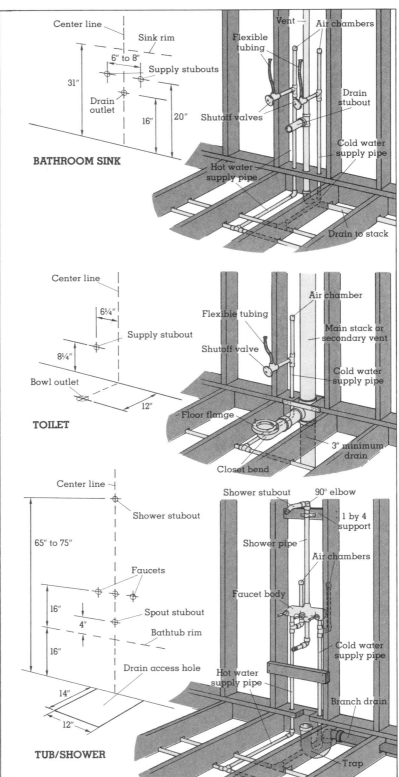

**Representative roughing-in measurements.** Plumbing components illustrated are a sink, toilet, and tub/shower. Use the measurements to help you plan; check local codes and specific fixture dimensions for exact roughing-in requirements.

# Electrical basics

What may appear to be a hopelessly tangled maze of wires running through the walls, under the floors, and above the ceiling of your home is actually a well-organized system composed of several electrical circuits. In your bathroom, those circuits supply power to light fixtures, switches, fans, heaters, and electrical outlets.

This section briefly explains your home's electrical system and offers general information about basic electrical improvements so you can better understand the processes involved in making changes to your electrical system. Techniques for installing light fixtures appear on pages 79–80.

Before you do any work yourself, talk with your building department's electrical inspector about local codes, the National Electrical Code (NEC), and your area's requirements for permits and inspections.

## Understanding your system

Today most homes have what's called "three-wire" service. The utility company connects three wires to your service entrance panel. Each of two hot wires supplies electricity at approximately 120 volts. A third wire—a neutral one—is maintained at zero volts. (Don't be misled, though; all three wires are live.)

Three-wire service provides both 120-volt and 240-volt capabilities. One hot wire and the neutral wire combine to provide 120 volts—primarily for lights and plug-in outlets. Two hot wires combine to provide 240 volts, often used for electric heaters.

**Service entrance panel.** This panel is the control center for your electrical system. Inside the panel, you'll usually find the main disconnect (main fuses or circuit breaker), the fuses or circuit breakers protecting each individual circuit, and the grounding connection for the entire system.

**Simple circuitry.** The word "circuit" means the course electric cur-

rent travels—in a continuous path from the service entrance panel or a separate subpanel, through one or more devices in your home that use electricity (such as light fixtures or appliances), and back to the panel. The devices are connected to the circuit by parallel wiring. With parallel wiring, a hot, a neutral, and a ground wire (for a 120-volt circuit) run continuously from one fixture box, outlet box, or switch box to another. Wires branch off to individual electrical devices from these continuous wires.

Modern circuit wires are housed together in a cable. Cable contains either one or two hot wires, a neutral wire, and a ground wire—each, except the ground wire, wrapped in its own insulation. (For the best connections, use only cable with all-copper wire.)

Individual wires are color-coded for easy identification. Hot wires are usually black or red, but may be any color other than white, gray, or green. Neutral wires are white or gray. Grounding wires are bare copper or green.

Occasionally, a white wire will be used as a hot wire; it should be taped or painted black near terminals and splices for easy identification.

**Grounding.** The NEC requires that every circuit have a ground wire. It provides an auxiliary path to ground for any short that might occur in a fixture or appliance. Also, according to the NEC, all bathroom outlets within 6 feet of a water source (sink or tub) must be protected with

ground fault circuit interrupters (GFCI). These cut off power within $\frac{1}{40}$ of a second if current begins leaking anywhere along the circuit. They may be special circuit breakers or built into an outlet.

## Extending a circuit

To extend an existing electrical circuit, you'll need a knack for making wire connections, and the patience to route new cable.

Before you start work, remember: NEVER WORK ON ANY LIVE CIRCUIT, FIXTURE, PLUG-IN OUTLET, OR SWITCH. Your life may depend on it. Turn off the circuit breaker or remove the fuse and make sure no one but you can turn the electricity back on.

The steps in extending a circuit are outlined below. Generally, you route new cable from box to box; you install new boxes where you want to add outlets, fixtures, or switches; and then you tap into a power source —an existing outlet, switch, or fixture box.

To install a new circuit, the work is much the same, except that you connect into a service panel or subpanel instead of into an existing outlet, switch, or fixture box.

**Select a power source.** A circuit can be tapped for power at almost any accessible outlet, switch, or fixture box of the appropriate voltage. (The exceptions are a switch box without a neutral wire and a fixture box at the end of a circuit.) The box you tap into must be large enough to hold new wires in addition to exist-

## ROUTING CABLE TO OUTLETS

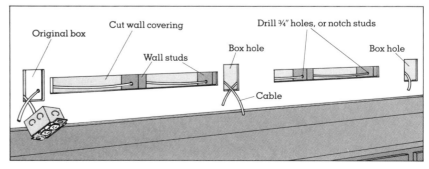

Original box · Cut wall covering · Wall studs · Drill ¾" holes, or notch studs · Box hole · Box hole · Cable

ing wires, and must have knockout holes through which you can run the new cable.

**Select and locate new boxes.** If wall or ceiling coverings have not yet been installed, choose an outlet or switch box you nail to studs or joists. If wall or ceiling coverings are already in place, choose cut-in boxes that don't have to be secured to studs or joists. Requirements regarding boxes for mounting ceiling fixtures are outlined on pages 79–80.

Unless codes prohibit the use of plastic, you can use either plastic or metal boxes. Metal boxes, though sturdier, must be grounded; plastic boxes cost less and need not be grounded, though the circuit must have a ground wire.

To find a suitable box location, first turn off power to all circuits that may be behind the wall or ceiling. Drill a small test hole and probe through it with a length of stiff insulated wire until you find an empty space.

Unless old boxes are at different levels, place new outlet boxes 12 to 18 inches above the floor, switch boxes or outlet boxes above a counter 44 inches above the floor. Never place boxes near a tub or shower.

If you're adding a new wall, you may be required by code to add an outlet every 12 feet, or one per wall regardless of the wall's length.

When you've determined the correct locations, trace the outline of each box on the wall or ceiling (omit protruding brackets). Then cut along the outlines.

**Route and connect new cable.** After the box holes are cut, run cable from the power source to each new box location. (Wait until you have the new boxes wired and the outlets, switches, and fixtures connected before you make the actual hookup to the source.)

Where you have access from an unfinished basement, an unfloored attic, or a garage adjacent to the bathroom, it's easy to run cable either attached to the joists or studs

or through holes drilled in them.

Where walls and ceilings are covered on both sides, you'll have to fish cable through them, using electrician's fish tape (illustrated below) or a length of stiff wire with one end bent into a blunt, tight hook.

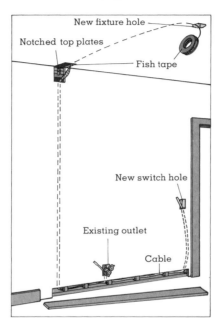

After routing new cable, secure the cable to each new box. Slip a cable connector onto the end of the cable and insert the cable and connector into a knockout in the box. Fasten the connector to the box, leaving 6 to 8 inches of cable sticking out for wiring connections. Then mount the box to the ceiling or wall and wire as described below.

**Wire plug-in outlets.** An outlet must have the same amperage and voltage rating as the circuit. If you have aluminum wiring, be sure to use the correct outlet; it will be identified by the letters CO-ALR. An outlet marked CU-AL should be used only with copper wire. If installing a GFCI outlet, follow the manufacturer's directions.

If you're adding a grounded outlet to a circuit that does not contain a grounding wire, you'll have to run a separate grounding wire from the new outlet to a nearby cold water pipe. (One method is shown on page 79; for help, consult an electrician.)

The drawing below shows how to wire a plug-in bathroom outlet with both halves live. The box is assumed to be metal; if you use a plastic box, there's no need to ground the box, but you'll have to attach a grounding wire to each outlet. Simply loop the end of the wire under the grounding screw. Connect the hot wire to the brass screw of the outlet, the neutral wire to the silver screw, and the ground wire to the green screw.

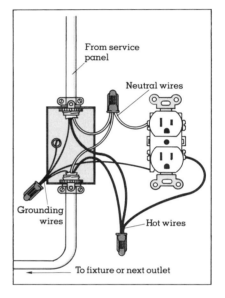

**Wire single-pole switches.** One single-pole switch may control one or more light fixtures, a heater, a ventilating fan, or several outlets.

Like outlets, the switch must have the same amperage and voltage rating as the circuit. If you have aluminum wiring, be sure to use a switch marked with the letters CO-ALR.

When wiring switches, remember that they are installed only on hot wires. The switches illustrated on page 78 have no grounding wires because the toggles on most home switches are made of shockproof plastic. If switches are housed in plastic boxes, the boxes do not need to be grounded. When installing a plastic switch box at the end of a circuit, secure the end of the grounding wire between the switch bracket and the mounting screw. If the switch is in the middle of a circuit,

# ■ Electrical basics

## WIRING SINGLE-POLE SWITCHES

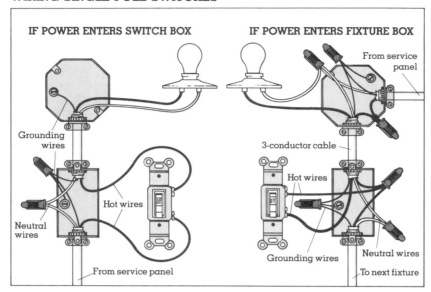

IF POWER ENTERS SWITCH BOX

IF POWER ENTERS FIXTURE BOX

From service panel

Grounding wires

3-conductor cable

Hot wires

Neutral wires

Hot wires

Grounding wires

Neutral wires

From service panel

To next fixture

## WIRING A GFCI

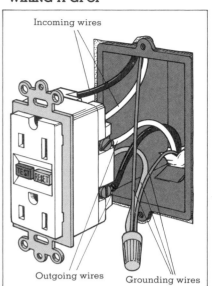

Incoming wires

TEST RESET

Outgoing wires

Grounding wires

just twist the ends of the ground wires together and cover them with a wirenut.

Single-pole switches have two screw terminals of the same color (usually brass) for wire connections, and a definite right-side up. You should be able to read the words ON and OFF embossed on the toggle. It makes no difference which hot wire goes to which terminal. The cable can be run first either to the fixture or to the switch—whichever is the more convenient route.

**Wire a GFCI.** The protection value of an outlet-style GFCI has made it standard in new construction. Depending on the model, the GFCI may also protect all other devices downstream (away from the source) from it, but it will not protect any outlets upstream (toward the source).

A GFCI receptacle is wired like an ordinary outlet, except that you must connect incoming hot and neutral wires to the "line," or input, terminals, and any outgoing wires to the "load" side. If your model in-

cludes a built-in grounding jumper, attach it to the other ground wires in the box with a wirenut, as shown above.

**Wire into the power source.** After you've wired new outlets and switches, you're ready to make the final connections. Connections to three types of boxes used as power sources are illustrated below. Wirenuts join and protect the stripped ends of spliced wires within the boxes.

## WIRING INTO A POWER SOURCE

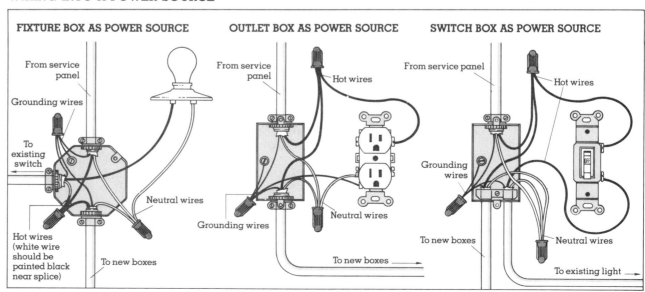

FIXTURE BOX AS POWER SOURCE

From service panel

Grounding wires

To existing switch

Neutral wires

Hot wires (white wire should be painted black near splice)

To new boxes

OUTLET BOX AS POWER SOURCE

From service panel

Hot wires

Grounding wires

Neutral wires

To new boxes

SWITCH BOX AS POWER SOURCE

From service panel

Hot wires

Grounding wires

To new boxes

Neutral wires

To existing light

## Installing light fixtures

Most bathrooms need both task lighting for specific areas and general lighting. For a discussion of lighting choices, see page 50.

Basically, to replace an existing light fixture with one of the same type, you disconnect the wires of the old fixture and hook up new wires. Adding a new fixture where there was none before is more complicated. You must first run new cable from a power source and install a fixture box and a switch.

Below are instructions for installing two types of light fixtures—surface-mounted and recessed.

### Surface-mounted fixtures. At-
tach these fixtures directly to a wall or ceiling fixture box, or suspend ceiling fixtures from a fixture box by chains or cord. New fixtures usually come with their own mounting hardware, adaptable to any fixture box.

Sometimes, though, the weight of the new fixture or the wiring necessary for proper grounding requires that you replace the box before installing the fixture.

Electrical code requirements sometimes allow ceiling fixtures weighing less than 24 ounces to be mounted on cut-in boxes held in position by the ceiling material. For a more secure installation and for heavier fixtures, you must fasten the box to a framing member or a special bracket secured to the joists. Do not attach fixtures heavier than 6 pounds to the box with screws through the fixture's metal canopy; use the hardware supplied by the manufacturer or check with your electrical inspector.

The NEC requires that all incandescent and fluorescent fixtures with exposed metal parts be grounded. If the fixture box is not grounded (as is the case when your present house wiring includes no grounding wire), you'll have to extend a grounding wire from the box to the nearest cold water pipe, as shown above right. The pipe must be metal, unbroken by plastic fittings or runs along its length. Bypass a problem spot or your water meter with a "jumper" wire. It's a good idea to ask a licensed electrician or building inspector to check your work.

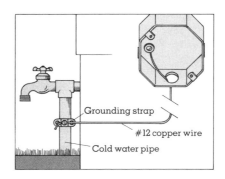

Grounding strap
#12 copper wire
Cold water pipe

A cord or chain-hung fixture must also have a grounding wire run from the socket to the box. Most new fixtures are prewired with a grounding wire.

Then install your new surface-mounted fixture as described below.

■ **To replace an existing fixture with a new one,** first turn off the circuit. Remove the shade, if any, from the

## SURFACE-MOUNTED FIXTURES

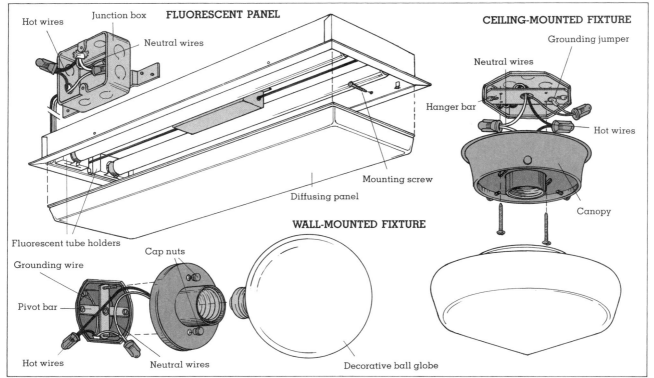

Hot wires
Junction box
**FLUORESCENT PANEL**
Neutral wires
**CEILING-MOUNTED FIXTURE**
Grounding jumper
Neutral wires
Hanger bar
Hot wires
Mounting screw
Diffusing panel
Canopy
Fluorescent tube holders
Cap nuts
**WALL-MOUNTED FIXTURE**
Grounding wire
Pivot bar
Hot wires
Neutral wires
Decorative ball globe

# ▪ Electrical basics

old fixture. Unscrew the canopy from the fixture box, and detach the mounting bar if there is one. Now make a sketch of how the wires are connected. If the wires are spliced with wirenuts, unscrew them and untwist the wires. If the wires are spliced and wrapped with electrician's tape, simply unwind the tape and untwist the wires.

Match the wires of the new fixture to the old wires shown in your sketch, and splice with wirenuts. Secure the new fixtures as recommended by the manufacturer, using any new hardware included.

▪ **To install a fixture in a new location,** you must route a new cable from a power source and install new fixture and switch boxes. New cable routed to the fixture box should include a grounding wire to be attached to the box's grounding screw. If more than one cable enters the box (for example, a separate cable from the switch box), you'll need to attach the end of a short length of bare 12-gauge wire (a "jumper") to the grounding screw, and use a wirenut to splice the other end to the ends of the grounding wires in the cables.

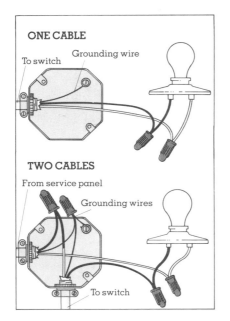

**RECESSED DOWNLIGHTS**

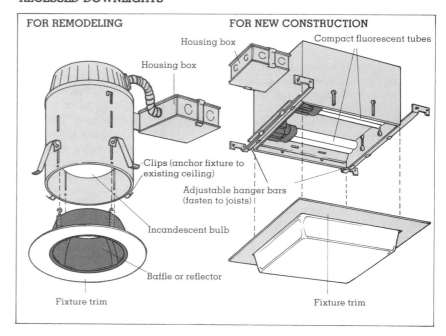

FOR REMODELING — Housing box, Housing box, Clips (anchor fixture to existing ceiling), Incandescent bulb, Baffle or reflector, Fixture trim

FOR NEW CONSTRUCTION — Compact fluorescent tubes, Adjustable hanger bars (fasten to joists), Fixture trim

Once you've routed the new cable and grounded the fixture box, wire in the new fixture—black wire to black, white to white; cap all splices with wirenuts. Then mount the fixture with hardware supplied by the manufacturer.

**Recessed ceiling fixtures.** Common recessed fixtures include incandescent circular or square downlights and larger fluorescent ceiling, or "troffer," panels. You'll need to cut a hole in the ceiling between the joists, or remove tiles or panels from a suspended ceiling, to install either type. Larger troffer panels may also require 2 by 4 blocking between joists for support.

Recessed fixtures need several inches of clearance above the finished ceiling. They're most easily installed below an unfinished attic or crawlspace. Because of the heat generated by many downlights, you must either buy a special zero-clearance model (type ICT), or plan to remove insulation within 3 inches of the fixture and make sure that no other combustible materials come within ½ inch.

Most low-voltage downlights come with an integral transformer

attached to the frame; if yours doesn't, you'll first need to mount an external transformer nearby and then route wire to the fixture.

If there's no crawlspace above the ceiling, find the joists (see page 68); don't forget to shut off power to any circuits that might be wired behind the ceiling before drilling exploratory holes.

Once you've determined the proper location for the fixture housing, trace its outline on the ceiling with a pencil; use a keyhole saw or saber saw to cut the hole. Brace a plaster ceiling as you cut.

If you don't have access from above, look for a remodeling fixture. The version shown above, at left, slips through the ceiling hole and clips onto the edge of the ceiling. The fixture trim then snaps onto the housing from below. (Hook up the wires to the circuit before securing the fixture and trim.)

So-called new work or rough-in downlights with adjustable hanger bars, such as the model shown above, at right, are easy to install from above. Simply nail the ends of the bars to joists on either side; then clip the trim or baffle into place from below.

# CLIMATE CONTROL: HEATING & VENTILATION

Certain elements of your bathroom's climate—steam, excess heat, early morning chill—can be annoying and unpleasant. When you remodel, consider adding an exhaust fan to freshen the air and draw out destructive moisture, and a heater to warm you on cool days. Installing these climate controllers is within the grasp of most do-it-yourselfers. For more details on both fans and heaters, see page 61.

## Heating the bathroom

Because electric heaters are easy to install and clean to operate, they're the most popular choice for heating bathrooms. In addition to the standard wall and ceiling-mounted units, you'll find heaters combined with exhaust fans, lights, or both. Many units require a dedicated 120 or 240-volt circuit, so shop carefully.

Gas heaters that can be recessed into a wall between two studs are available in a variety of styles and sizes. Regardless of how they heat, all gas models require a gas supply line and must be vented to the outside.

Choose the location of your heater carefully. Of course, you'll want to place it where someone getting out of the tub or shower will benefit from it (this is particularly true of radiant heaters, which heat objects directly). But don't locate the heater where someone will bump against its hot surfaces, or where it might char or ignite curtains or towels.

Since gas heaters require a vent to the outside, you'll probably want to place the heater on an outside wall. Otherwise, you'll have to run the vent through the attic or crawlspace and out through the roof. It's best to have a professional run gas lines; in any case, you must have the work tested and inspected before the gas is turned on.

## Ventilating the bathroom

You can buy fans to mount in the wall or in the ceiling. Some models are combined with a light or a heater; some have both.

It's important that your exhaust fan have adequate capacity. The Home Ventilating Institute (HVI) rec-

ommends that the fan be capable of exchanging the air at least eight times every hour. To determine the required fan capacity in cubic feet per minute (CFM) for a bathroom with an 8-foot ceiling, multiply the room's length and width in feet by 1.1.

For example, if your bathroom is 6 by 9 feet, you would calculate the required fan capacity as follows:

$$6 \times 9 \times 1.1 = 59.4 \text{ CFM}$$

Rounding off, you would need fan capacity of at least 60 CFM. If your fan must exhaust through a long duct or several elbows, you'll need greater capacity to overcome the increased resistance. Follow the dealer's or manufacturer's recommendations.

Ideally, your fan should be mounted as close to the shower or tub as possible. It should also be as far away as possible from the source of replacement air (the door, for instance). In addition, you'll want the exhaust duct to be as short and straight as possible. If you have trouble finding a location that meets all three requirements, you may want to consult a professional.

## THREE WAYS TO DUCT EXHAUST FANS

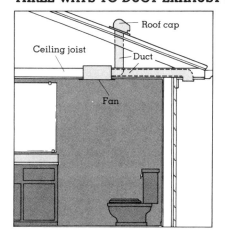

**Ceiling fan** ventilates through duct either to roof cap on roof or to grill in soffit under the eave.

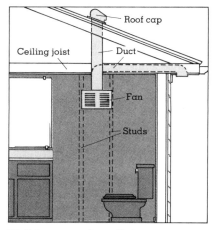

**Wall fan on inside wall** also ventilates through duct to cap on roof or to grill in soffit under the eave.

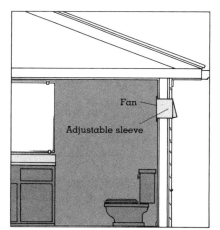

**Wall fan on outside wall,** installed between wall studs, ventilates through wall directly to outside.

# Sinks

Replacing the bathroom sink (also known as a lavatory or basin) is one of the quickest ways to give your bathroom a new look without getting involved in a complex and expensive remodeling project.

This section will show you how to remove and install the four basic types of sinks: integral sink and countertop, pedestal, wall-hung, and deck-mount. For more information on the many sink models and materials, see page 56.

If you're planning to add a sink or to move one, you may want to consult a professional about extending supply, drain, and vent lines (see pages 72–75). But to replace a sink, extensive experience with plumbing isn't a requirement.

## REMOVING A SINK

Unless you're installing a new floor covering, be sure to protect the bathroom floor with a piece of cardboard or plywood before you begin work. You'll also want a bucket and a supply of rags or sponges nearby to soak up excess water.

To loosen corroded plumbing connections, douse them with penetrating oil an hour before you start.

### Disconnecting the plumbing

If the sink faucet is mounted on the countertop and you don't plan to replace the faucet, it isn't necessary to disconnect the water supply lines. If the faucet is connected to the sink, you do need to disconnect the supply lines.

Be sure to turn off the water at the sink shutoff valves or at the main valve before doing any work. Disconnect the supply lines at the shutoff valves, placing a bucket underneath them to catch any water, and open the faucets so the lines can drain.

If your sink isn't equipped with shutoff valves, disconnect the supply lines at the faucet inlet shanks, as explained on page 92—and plan to add shutoff valves before you connect the plumbing to the new sink (or

have a professional plumber do the work for you).

Next, move the bucket underneath the trap. If the trap has a cleanout plug, remove it to drain the water, then loosen the slip nuts and remove the trap. If there is no cleanout plug, remove the trap and dump the water into the bucket.

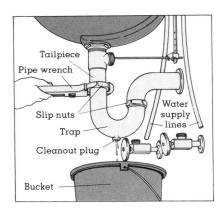

Disconnect the pop-up drain assembly by loosening the clevis screw and then removing the spring clip that connects the stopper and pivot rod to the pop-up rod on the faucet (see "Removing a sink faucet," page 92).

The tailpiece, drain body, and sink flange, as well as the faucet, will now come out with the sink. If you plan to reuse the old faucet, remove it carefully from the sink and set aside.

### Removing an integral sink & countertop

An integral sink is molded as part of the countertop, and the unit is secured to the top of a vanity cabinet. Look underneath for any metal clips or wooden braces securing the unit, and remove them. Then lift off the whole unit.

If you can't remove the unit easily, insert the end of a small prybar in the joint between the countertop and vanity cabinet at a back corner. Carefully lift up the prybar to break the sealing material between the countertop and the vanity. If the joint is too narrow to accept the end of a prybar, cut through the sealing ma-

terial with a hot putty knife, then pry or lift up the countertop.

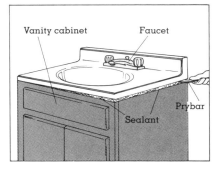

### Removing a pedestal sink

Most pedestal sinks are made of two pieces—the sink and the pedestal or base. Look in the opening at the rear of the pedestal to locate a nut or bolt holding the sink down. If you find one, remove it. Lift off the sink and set it aside.

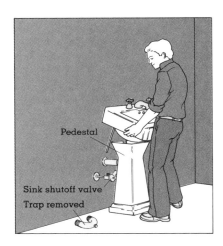

The pedestal is usually bolted to the floor. You may find the bolts on the base, or on the inside of the pedestal (see illustration above right). Undo the bolts and remove the pedestal. If you can't move it after removing the bolts, rock it back and forth, and then lift it out. If the pedestal is recessed into a ceramic tile floor, you may have to remove the surrounding floor tiles with a cold chisel and soft-headed steel hammer. Rock the pedestal back and forth to break any remaining seal with the floor. Lift the pedestal up and set it aside.

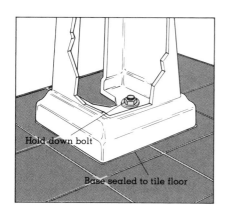

Hold-down bolt

Base sealed to tile floor

## Removing a wall-hung sink

To remove a wall-hung sink, first unscrew the legs, if any, that support the front of the sink. Check underneath for any bolts securing the sink to the mounting bracket on the wall (see illustration below), and remove them. Then lift the sink straight up and off the mounting bracket.

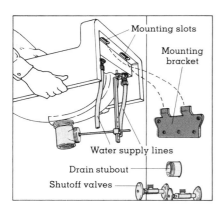

Mounting slots

Mounting bracket

Water supply lines

Drain stubout

Shutoff valves

## Removing a deck-mount sink

There are three basic types of deck-mount sinks used in vanity countertops: self-rimming or rimless sinks, flush-mount sinks, and unrimmed or recessed sinks. All may be secured to the countertop with lugs or clamps that must be unscrewed before you remove the sink.

### Self-rimming or rimless sinks.

These have a molded flange that sits on the countertop. Once you have removed any lugs or clamps from underneath, just use a hot putty knife or other knife to cut through the

sealing material between sink and countertop; then pry up the sink to break the seal and lift it out.

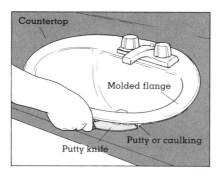

Countertop

Molded flange

Putty or caulking

Putty knife

### Flush-mount sinks.

Have a helper support the sink while you undo the lugs or clamps that secure the sink's metal rim to the countertop. (If you're working alone, you can support the sink with a 2 by 4 and a wood block tied together through the drain; see illustration below.) After you remove the lugs or clamps, cut through the sealing material between the rim and the countertop with a hot putty knife or other knife. Pry up the rim to free the sink; then lift straight up.

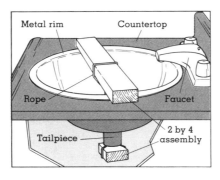

Metal rim

Countertop

Rope

Faucet

Tailpiece

2 by 4 assembly

### Unrimmed or recessed sinks.

An unrimmed or recessed sink is secured to the underside of the countertop. The easiest way to remove the sink is to first take off the countertop. Check underneath for any brackets and remove them. Then insert a prybar into the joint between the countertop and the vanity cabinet near a rear corner, and pry up. Turn the countertop bottom side up and rest it on a padded surface. Undo the lugs or clamps securing the sink, and lift it off the countertop.

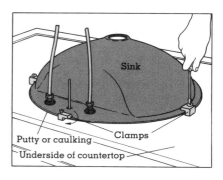

Sink

Putty or caulking

Clamps

Underside of countertop

When the countertop is tiled, the flange usually rests on top of the plywood base for the tile. Look underneath; if you don't see any clips or brackets, you'll have to remove the tile surrounding the edge of the sink. With a soft-headed steel hammer and cold chisel, remove enough tile so that you can lift the sink from the countertop. (Be sure to protect your eyes with goggles.) If you can't find matching replacement tile and need to reuse the old tiles, remove them carefully to avoid breaking them.

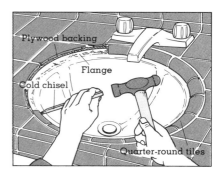

Plywood backing

Flange

Cold chisel

Quarter-round tiles

## INSTALLING A SINK

If you're installing a sink at a new location instead of replacing an existing one, you'll need to extend the supply, drain, and vent pipes (see pages 72–75).

If you'd like your sink to be higher than standard, you can raise the vanity of an integral or deck-mount sink by building a base under it. If you're installing a wall-hung sink, simply mount the bracket higher. You can't adjust the height of a pedestal sink, but you may be able to buy a taller model.

*(Continued on next page)*

# ∎Sinks

### MOUNTING A DUAL-HANDLE FAUCET

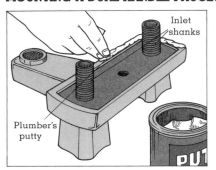

**Apply putty** to bottom edge of the faucet if there is no rubber gasket to seal it to sink's surface.

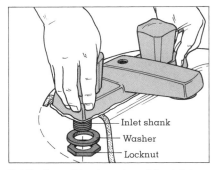

**Set the faucet** in place, insert the inlet shanks through the sink holes, and press down. Add washers and locknuts.

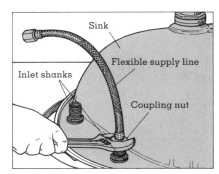

**Attach flexible supply lines** to the faucet's inlet shanks, using pipe joint compound and coupling nuts.

Before installing the sink, you'll need to install the faucet and the sink flange.

## Installing the faucet & sink flange

Whether the faucet is to be mounted on the countertop or on the sink itself, you'll find it easier to install the faucet before you set the sink in place. The main steps are illustrated above. First make sure that the mounting surface is clean. If your faucet came with a rubber gasket, place it on the bottom of the faucet. For a faucet without a gasket, put a bead of plumber's putty around the bottom edge of the faucet.

Set the faucet in position, and press it down onto the sink or countertop surface. Assemble the washers and locknuts on the inlet shanks, and then tighten the nuts. Remove excess putty from around the faucet. Connect the supply lines to the inlet shanks and tighten the coupling nuts. For more information on installing faucets, see pages 92–93.

Now install the sink flange and drain. To attach the flange, run a bead of plumber's putty around the drain hole of the sink. Press the flange into the puttied hole. Put the locknut, metal washer, and flat rubber washer on the drain body in that order. Insert the threaded end of the drain body into the bottom of the sink and screw it onto the flange. Then tighten the locknut until it is snug (do not overtighten).

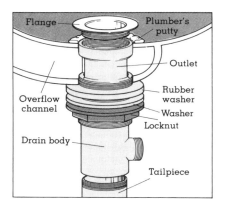

## Installing an integral sink & countertop

Cover the top edges of the vanity cabinet with a sealant recommended by the manufacturer. Place the countertop unit on the cabinet flush with the back edge. Make sure the overhang—if any—is equal on the left and right. Press along the countertop edges to complete the seal, and check around the perimeter, removing any excess sealant.

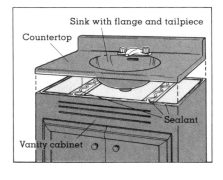

If your unit came with mounting brackets, use them to secure the countertop to the vanity. Seal the joint between the countertop and the wall with caulking compound.

## Installing a pedestal sink

Position a *dual-handle faucet* as shown above. Assemble the washers and locknuts on the inlet shanks; then tighten the nuts. Remove excess putty from around the faucet. Connect the supply lines to the inlet shanks.

Most *single-lever faucets* include short supply tubes; simply tighten the locknuts on the threaded stubs from below. For details, see pages 92–93.

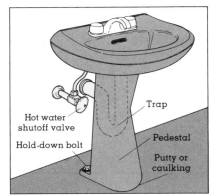

Position the sink on top of the pedestal and, if required by the manufacturer, bolt the two together as directed.

## Installing a wall-hung sink

For new installations, you'll need to remove the wall coverings and wallboard. Notch two studs directly behind the sink's proposed location, and nail or screw a 1 by 6 or 1 by 8 mounting board flush to the stud fronts; then re-cover the wall.

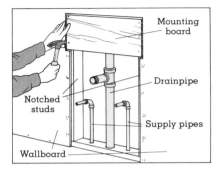

Mounting board
Drainpipe
Notched studs
Supply pipes
Wallboard

Before you attach the mounting bracket to the wall mounting board, check to see that it fits the sink. Refer to the manufacturer's instructions to properly position the bracket. Generally, you center the bracket over the drainpipe, then level it at the desired height from the floor. Fasten the bracket to the mounting board with woodscrews, making sure that it's level. Then carefully lower the sink onto the mounting bracket.

Because the mounting bracket can bend or break under the weight of a large wall-hung sink, the manufacturer may recommend that adjustable legs be inserted into the holes under the front corners of the sink. Screw the legs down until the sink is level; be sure to keep the legs plumb.

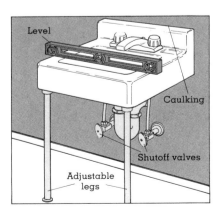

Level
Caulking
Shutoff valves
Adjustable legs

Seal the joint between the back of the sink and the wall with caulking compound.

## Installing a deck-mount sink

If your countertop doesn't have a hole for the sink, you'll need to cut one. For a self-rimming or an unrimmed sink, mark the hole, using the templates supplied with the sink. If you didn't receive a template, cut one from paper; it should fit loosely around the outside of the sink bowl where the bowl meets the flange.

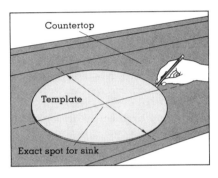

Countertop
Template
Exact spot for sink

For a flush-mount sink, trace the bottom edge of the sink's metal framing rim directly onto the spot where the sink will sit in the countertop.

After you mark the location of the cutout, drill a starting hole, then use a saber saw to cut the opening.

Install your deck-mount sink as described below.

### Self-rimming or rimless sinks.
First, run a bead of caulking compound or plumber's putty around the underside of the flange. Set the sink on the countertop and press it down until the putty oozes out. Install any lugs or clamps according to the manufacturer's instructions. Remove excess putty.

### Flush-mount sinks.
Apply a bead of caulking compound or plumber's putty around the sink lip. Fasten the metal framing rim around the lip, following the manufacturer's directions. Next, apply a bead of caulking compound or plumber's putty

around the top edge of the countertop sink opening, and set the sink and rim in place. Secure the sink and rim to the underside of the countertop with the lugs or clamps provided. Wipe off excess putty.

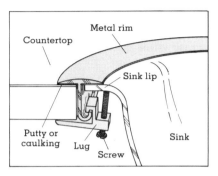

Metal rim
Countertop
Sink lip
Putty or caulking
Lug
Screw
Sink

### Unrimmed or recessed sinks.
Turn the countertop upside down and apply plumber's putty or caulking compound on the underside, around the edge of the sink opening. Set the sink in place, checking from the other side to be sure it is centered in the opening. Anchor the sink as recommended by the manufacturer. If you're finishing the countertop with ceramic tile, you can mount the sink atop the plywood base and then edge it with tile trim.

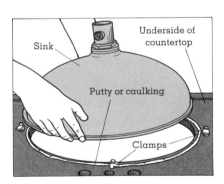

Sink
Underside of countertop
Putty or caulking
Clamps

## Connecting the plumbing

Once the sink is installed, connect the water supply lines to the shutoff valves and tighten the coupling nuts. Then connect the trap to the drainpipe and tailpiece, and tighten the slip nuts (see drawing, page 82). Connect the pop-up stopper to the faucet pop-up rod (see page 93). Turn on the water at the shutoff valves or main shutoff; check for leaks.

# Bathtubs

Installing or replacing a bathtub can be a complicated job—one that takes careful planning. But a gleaming new tub in your bathroom is well worth the effort.

Your tub choices range from porcelain-enameled cast iron or steel to lightweight fiberglass-reinforced plastic. The waterproof wall covering around a tub (called a surround) can be tile or panels of fiberglass-reinforced plastic or coated hardboard.

If you're building a new bathroom, you can create an entire bath area with a tub and surround manufactured as a one-piece unit. These units are not recommended for remodeling projects, though, since they are usually too large to fit through a door and must be moved in before the bathroom walls are framed. For remodeling, your best choice is a tub with separate wall panels or tiles.

Before you install a tub in a new location, check local building codes for support requirements; a bathtub filled with water is extremely heavy and needs plenty of support. You should also check the plumbing code requirements for extending the water supply and drain-waste and vent systems (see page 73). Consider getting professional help to build the framing and to rough-in plumbing for a new installation.

In this section, you'll find general directions for removing and installing bathtubs and wall coverings. For detailed product information, see page 57.

## REMOVING A BATHTUB

There are three main steps to this job: disconnecting the appropriate plumbing, removing part or all of the wall covering, and removing the tub itself.

### Disconnecting the plumbing

Generally it's not necessary to turn off the water unless you're replacing the faucet body. If you do need to turn off the water, do so at the fixture shutoff valves (if you can reach them through an access door in an adjoining room or hallway) or at the main shutoff valve. Open the faucets to drain the pipes.

Next, remove any fittings—spout, faucet parts, shower head, and diverter handle—that will be in the way. To remove the tub, you'll also have to unscrew and remove the overflow cover and drain lever. By pulling out this fitting, you'll also remove the bathtub drain assembly if it's a trip-lever type.

If you have a pop-up stopper, pull it out with the rocker linkage after removing the overflow cover (see illustration below).

If there's an access door or access from the basement or crawlspace, use a pipe wrench to loosen the coupling nuts from behind the tub; disconnect the trap and waste tee, as shown below, at right. If you can't get access to the drain plumbing, you can work from inside the tub; disconnect the tub from the overflow pipe and drainpipe by unscrewing the overflow retainer flange and drain flange.

### Removing the wall covering

Most bathtubs are recessed; that is, they are surrounded by walls on three sides. Depending on whether you want to replace the tub only, or the tub and the wall covering, you'll need to remove all or part of the surrounding tiles or panels. Before doing this, remove any fittings, such as the shower head, that are in the way (if you haven't yet done so).

**Tile.** If there are wall or floor tiles along the edge of the tub, free the tub by chipping out approximately 4 inches to the nearest grout joint (see illustration above right). On the walls, remove the plaster or gypsum wallboard backing at the same time, so that several inches of the wall studs are exposed. Use a cold chisel and soft-headed steel hammer to remove the tile, and be sure to protect your eyes from fragments by wearing goggles.

If you're removing a recessed tub, you must also remove enough tile (and other obstructions) from the floor and walls to be able to slide the tub out of its recess.

**Fiberglass panels.** Take out the wall panels by first removing the

## DISCONNECTING THE PLUMBING

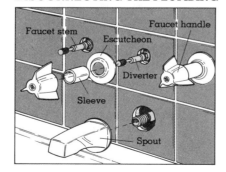

**Remove faucet and diverter parts** and spout, leaving stubout for spout and faucet and diverter stems.

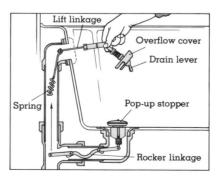

**Unscrew overflow cover,** then pull out drain assembly—first the overflow cover and lift linkage, then the pop-up stopper.

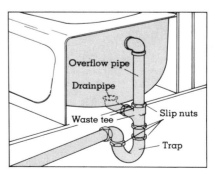

**Loosen slip nuts** and remove trap from underneath tub; then disconnect and remove overflow pipe.

REMODELING BASICS   **87**

## REMOVING WALL COVERINGS

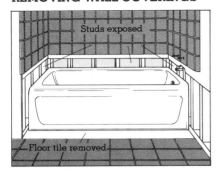

**For tile walls,** chip away a 4-inch strip of tile and backing from walls; remove an equivalent strip from a tile floor.

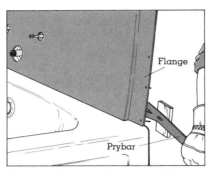

**For fiberglass panels,** pry panel flange and pull panel and any backing off the wall studs.

gypsum wallboard or molding from the panel flanges. With a prybar, pry the panels, along with any backing, off the studs. Once the end panels are removed, you can take out the back panel, leaving the exposed wall studs (see illustration above).

### Removing the tub

The tub's bulk will make this one of your biggest jobs. To get the tub out, you may first have to remove the bathroom door or even cut a hole in the wall opposite the tub plumbing. Plan exactly how you'll route the tub through and out of the house. You'll need helpers to move it, especially if it's a heavy steel or cast-iron fixture.

**Steel or cast-iron tubs.** Locate and remove from the wall studs any nails or screws at the top of the tub's flange (lip) that may be holding the tub in place. With at least one helper (probably three for a cast-iron tub), lift up the tub with a prybar and slide two or three soaped wooden runners under it (see illustration at right). Then slide the tub out of the recess.

**Fiberglass tubs.** To remove a fiberglass or plastic tub, pull out all nails or screws driven into the wall studs through the flange. Reach between the studs and grasp the tub under the flange (see illustration far right); with the aid of a helper, if necessary, pull the tub up off its supports and out of the recess.

---

## INSTALLING A BATHTUB

If you're replacing an old tub with a new one, carefully inspect the subfloor where the tub will be installed for level and for moisture damage, and make any necessary repairs or adjustments.

If you're installing a tub in a new location, you'll do the framing and rough-in the plumbing first (see "Structural basics," pages 67–70, and "Plumbing basics," pages 72–75).

### Setting, leveling & securing the tub

This is the most crucial part of the installation process. A tub must be correctly supported and carefully secured in a level position so that it will drain properly and all plumbing connections can be made easily.

## MOVING THE TUB

**To move a steel or cast-iron tub,** slide it across floor on soaped wooden runners. You'll need several helpers .

**Steel or cast-iron tubs.** These heavy tubs require either vertical or horizontal wood supports (see "Four ways to support a tub" on the following page). Horizontal supports are 1 by 4s or 2 by 4s, nailed across the wall studs so that the tub's flange rests on them. Vertical supports are 2 by 4s nailed to each stud. Position the supports so that the tub will be level both from end to end and from back to front.

If your tub is steel, you can attach prefabricated metal hangers to the studs with woodscrews to support the tub.

When you've attached the appropriate supports, slide your new tub along soaped wooden runners into position (see illustration below). With the aid of several helpers, lift it so that the flanges rest on the supports. Check the tub at both ends to see that it's level. If not, insert shims between the tub and wall supports or floor to level it. To prevent the tub from slipping, anchor it by driving nails or screws into the studs tight against the top of the flange.

**Fiberglass tubs.** If necessary, temporarily remove any protruding stubouts. Then, with a helper, set the tub on wood supports, tight against the rear studs.

Once the tub is in position, check on top for level at both ends, shimming where needed, as for steel and cast-iron models. Drill holes in the tub flange and carefully nail or screw through the holes into the studs.

*(Continued on next page)*

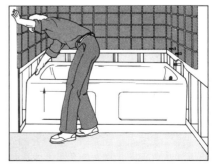

**To move a fiberglass tub,** grasp it under back of the flange and lift it up and out. A helper will make the job easier.

# ■Bathtubs

## Connecting the plumbing

Once the tub is secured in position, reconnect the overflow pipe, trap, and drain assembly. (Be careful not to overtighten the nuts and crack the tub's surface.) Make sure you connect the overflow pipe with the tub drainpipe on the side of the trap nearest the bathtub, not on the far side.

If you're reusing existing wall coverings, install the faucet and spout, plus a diverter and shower head as required. If you plan on a new wall covering (see below), connect the fittings afterwards.

## Installing the wall covering

Before patching or re-covering the walls with either tile or panels, turn on the water and check the drain and supply pipes for leaks.

If you plan to install a tiled wall, see pages 103–105. If you're starting from scratch, it's best to use cement backer board as a base.

To install new fiberglass panels, cover any exposed studs with gypsum wallboard (cut to accommodate the plumbing) or cement backer board. Then follow the procedure below.

**Drill pipe holes.** To install a panel over pipe stubouts and faucet and

## FOUR WAYS TO SUPPORT A TUB

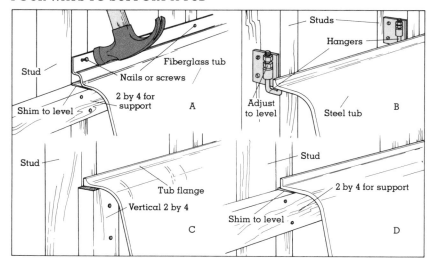

**Support a new tub** in one of these ways: nail or screw fiberglass tub flange to studs (A); support steel tub with metal hangers (B); nail vertical 2 by 4s to studs to support metal tubs (C); nail horizontal 2 by 4s to support metal tubs (D).

diverter stems, you'll need to mark and drill it accurately (see illustration below). Measure and mark the panel by holding it up against the stubouts and stems. Drill slightly oversized holes in the panel with a spade bit, backing the panel with a wood plank to prevent splintering.

**Set panels.** Apply mastic in S-patterns to the backs of the panels (see illustration below), and press

the panels in place around the top of the tub, according to manufacturer's directions. If panels are to be nailed or screwed to the studs, predrill all nail holes.

**Finish and seal panels.** Seal all gaps between the wall covering and the stubouts and stems with silicone caulk. Finally, attach the faucet and diverter parts, spout, and shower head.

## INSTALLING PANELS AROUND A TUB

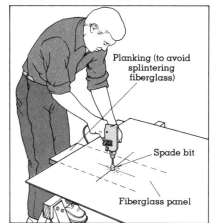

**After carefully marking** one panel to fit over the stubouts and faucet and diverter stems, drill holes in it with a spade bit.

**Apply mastic** to panel in S-patterns while panel rests on planks laid across a pair of sawhorses.

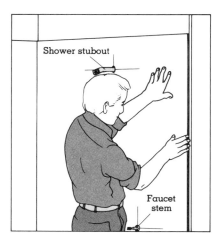

**Press panel** into place on the wall, fitting it over stubouts and faucet and diverter stems.

# Showers

From elegant ceramic tile to easy-to-install fiberglass or plastic panels, your choices are many when it comes to replacing or adding a shower in your home. And if you're installing a completely new bathroom, you can also choose a molded one-piece shower enclosure. (These are not recommended for remodeling projects because they won't fit through most bathroom doors.)

In this section you'll find instructions for removing all types of showers (including the older metal units) and for installing tile and fiberglass-reinforced or plastic-paneled showers. For more details on the various models, see page 58.

## REMOVING A SHOWER

Most showers consist of three walls with waterproof wall covering, such as tile or panels, and a separate base, mounted in a wood frame. Removing a shower is a three-step procedure: disconnecting the plumbing, removing the wall covering, and removing the base. If the shower is a one-piece unit, you'll also have to cut a hole in a wall to get it out, unless you cut the unit into pieces.

If you're changing the location of a shower or permanently removing it, you'll probably want to dismantle the wood frame and remove the plumbing.

### Disconnecting the plumbing

First remove the shower door or the rod and curtain. Then turn off the water supply at the fixture shutoff valves (sometimes accessible through an access door in an adjoining hallway or closet) or at the main shutoff valve. Open the faucets to drain the pipes. Then sponge the shower base dry.

Remove the faucet handles and other trim parts, leaving the faucet stems. Then remove the shower head with a pipe wrench tape-wrapped to avoid scarring the fixture (see illustration above).

## DISCONNECTING SHOWER PLUMBING

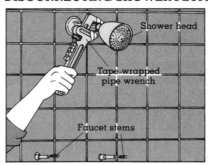

**Use pipe wrench** wrapped with tape to remove shower head. (Faucet parts have already been removed.)

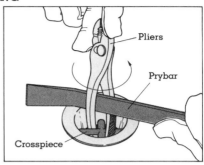

**After removing** drain cover, use pliers and prybar to unscrew crosspiece from drain.

Unscrew and pry up the drain cover, and with a pair of pliers and a small prybar, unscrew the crosspiece (see illustration). If you're removing a one-piece shower enclosure, you'll also have to disconnect the drainpipe and remove protruding faucet stems and fittings that might get in the way when you tip the unit to pull it out. Finally, plug the drain opening with a rag to prevent debris from falling into it.

### Removing the wall covering

The removal procedure you'll follow depends on whether you have a tiled

shower, walls covered with fiberglass panels, or an older metal shower.

After you've removed the wall covering, check for moisture damage to the frame and to any soundproofing insulation secured across the inside of the frame. Repair or replace if necessary.

**Tile.** Ceramic tile is the most difficult wall covering to remove. If the existing tile is clean, smooth, and securely attached, you can avoid removing it by using it as a backing for a new tile surface. If you must remove it, proceed with caution and wear goggles while you work.

*(Continued on next page)*

## REMOVING SHOWER WALLS

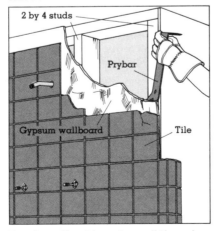

**For tile walls,** chip and pry off tile and wallboard backing to expose entire frame of shower.

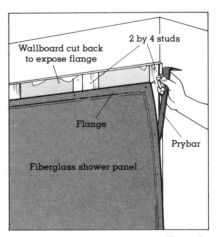

**For panel walls,** remove any wallboard or molding covering panel flanges; then pry panels off frame.

# ■ Showers

To remove tile set in mortar, you must break up the tile, mortar, and any backing with a sledge hammer. Remove it down to the wood frame, being careful not to hit and damage the wall studs. You may want to hire a tile professional for this part of the project.

If the tile is set on wallboard with adhesive, use a cold chisel and soft-headed steel hammer to chip away small sections of tile and backing. Then insert a prybar and pry off large sections of tile and backing until the entire frame is exposed (see illustration, page 89).

**Fiberglass panels.** First remove any molding or wallboard covering the panel flanges. Then pry panels, along with any backing and nails, off the wood frame (see illustration, page 89). If you're removing a one-piece enclosure, you may have to cut it apart to get it out (a saber saw with a plastic-cutting blade will do the job quickly).

**Metal showers.** Remove metal shower walls by unscrewing them at the edges and then at the front and back corners. These screws hold the shower walls to each other and sometimes to a wood frame. If the screws are rusted, cut the screw heads off with a hacksaw or cold chisel; then separate the walls with a hard pull.

## Removing the base

The base may be tile on a mortar bed, or it may be a fiberglass unit. Tile is difficult to remove because it's laid in mortar; fiberglass bases are simply pried out.

After you've removed the base, inspect the subfloor and framing for moisture damage, and repair where necessary.

**Tile on mortar.** As with tile walls, check first to see if you can lay the new tile over the old. If not, use a sledge hammer to break up and remove all tile and mortar down to the subfloor. You may be able to pry up one side of the base and slip a

wedge under it to make it easier to break up. Wear goggles to protect your eyes from tile or mortar fragments.

**Fiberglass.** Remove all nails or screws from the flange around the top of the base. Pry the base off the floor with a prybar; lift it out.

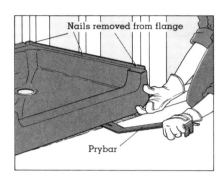

Nails removed from flange

Prybar

---

## INSTALLING A SHOWER

When you replace an old shower, the plumbing—and probably the wood frame—will already be in place.

If you're putting a shower in a new location, you must first frame the shower walls using 2 by 4s (see "Structural basics," pages 67–70). Make accurate measurements (follow the manufacturer's directions to frame a fiberglass shower); keep framing square and plumb.

Once the frame is complete, you'll also need to rough-in supply and drain lines, and install the faucet and pipe for the shower head (see pages 72–75 and 94).

Now you're ready to install the shower—first the base, then the walls.

## Installing the base

Installing a watertight tiled base on a mortar bed is a highly complicated project not recommended for beginners. If you want this type of base in either a tile or panel shower, consider having a professional build it.

To install a fiberglass or plastic base, position it over the drain outlet. Connect the base to the drain by screwing in the crosspiece (see il-

lustration, page 89), and cover the opening with rags to keep debris from falling in. Follow the manufacturer's directions to secure the base to the frame (nailing is shown below). Later, remove the rags and attach the drain cover.

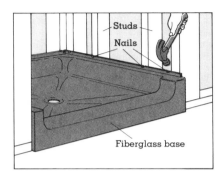

Studs

Nails

Fiberglass base

## Installing the wall covering

Once the base is secured, you're ready to cover the shower's side and back walls with tile or panels.

**Tile.** Like a tile base, tile walls can be tricky to install. If you want tile on a mortar bed, you may want to hire a tile contractor to install it. If you're planning to back the tile with either water-resistant wallboard or cement backer board, you may decide to do the job yourself.

First, prepare the backing. Cut holes for the shower head stubout and faucet stems; then nail the backing to the frame (see illustration above right).

Plan the layout of your tile by marking horizontal and vertical working lines on the shower wall (see illustrations above right). Using thin-set adhesive, tile the back wall. Then move on to the sides, cutting tiles to fit around the shower stubout and faucet stems.

Set ceramic tile accessories. Allow the tile to set (for the required time, consult the adhesive manufacturer's instructions) before grouting all the joints between the tiles. When the grout has set, you can seal it. For more information on establishing working lines, setting tile, and grouting joints, turn to pages 103–105; or ask your tile dealer.

## INSTALLING TILE ON SHOWER WALLS

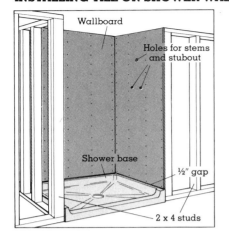

**To attach wallboard** or backer board to a wood shower frame, nail along the length of the 2 by 4 studs.

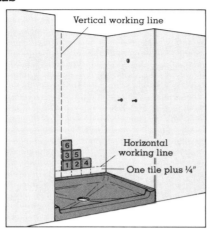

**Mark working lines,** both horizontal and vertical, then set tile on shower walls in a pyramid pattern.

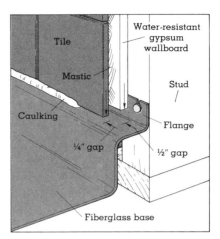

**Backing** is positioned to leave ½-inch gap above base; leave ¼-inch gap for caulking tile.

**Fiberglass panels.** Shower panels of fiberglass usually come with manufacturer's directions for installation. Some require no backing (except perhaps soundproofing insulation); others require separate water-resistant wallboard backing.

For both types of panels, measure and mark on one panel the locations of the shower head stubout and faucet stems. Lay the marked panel across two sawhorses, and with a spade bit, drill slightly oversized holes for your fittings. Support the panels with wood planks so you don't splinter them as you drill (see illustration below).

If the base of your shower has channels on the outside edges for sealant, clean out any debris from them. Then fill the groove at the back with the sealant recommended by the manufacturer (see illustration below). Also apply adhesive to the reverse side of the back panel according to manufacturer's directions.

Install the back panel by fitting it into the groove on the base, then pressing it against the frame to make a complete seal. Next, fill the other grooves on the base with seal-

ant and install the side panels; they may snap or clip to the back panel. Screw or nail the flanges of the panels to the framing. Install cover moldings over the nails or screws, if required.

### Connecting the plumbing

Once you've installed the wall coverings, caulk around all openings; then re-attach the shower head, escutcheons, and faucet handles.

Finally, hang the shower door, or mount a curtain rod and hang a shower curtain.

## INSTALLING FIBERGLASS SHOWER PANELS

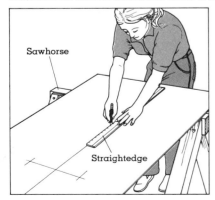

**Mark a panel** for stubout hole and faucet stem, set panel on supporting planks and sawhorses, and drill holes.

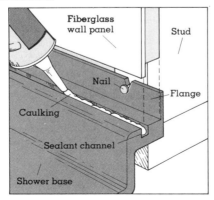

**Channel in shower base** holds panel tightly in place; sealant prevents moisture from getting behind panels.

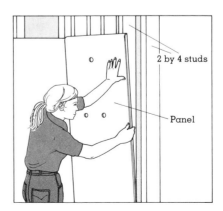

**Press panel to the frame,** guiding head stubout and faucet stems through holes; nail or screw panel flange to frame.

# Faucets

Whether you're replacing an old faucet or selecting fittings for a new sink or bathtub, you'll find a wide variety of faucet types and styles from which to choose. The product information on page 59 can help you make your selection.

In this section, you'll find information on removing and installing two different types of widely used bathroom faucets: deck-mount models for sinks, and wall-mount models for bathtubs and showers.

## SINK FAUCETS

In choosing a deck-mount faucet, be sure that the faucet's inlet shanks are spaced to fit the holes in your sink. If you're replacing a faucet, it's wise to take the old one with you when you shop. You'll also need new water supply lines, so take them with you, too.

Choose a unit that comes with clear installation instructions, and make sure that repair kits or replacement parts are readily available.

### Removing a sink faucet

Before removing the faucet, turn off the water at the sink shutoff valves or main shutoff valve. Place a bucket under the valves and use a wrench to remove the coupling nuts connecting the water supply lines to the valves. Open the faucet and allow the water to drain from the lines.

If your sink has a pop-up drain, you'll need to disconnect it before removing the faucet. Unfasten the clevis screw and spring clip that secure the pivot rod to the pop-up rod, and remove the pop-up rod from the faucet body (see drawing on facing page).

With an adjustable or basin wrench, reach up behind the sink and remove the coupling nuts holding the supply lines to the inlet shanks on the faucet (see illustration above). Use the wrench to remove the locknuts from the shanks. Take off the washers; then lift up the faucet and remove it from the sink or countertop.

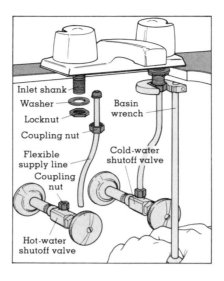

Inlet shank
Washer
Locknut
Coupling nut
Flexible supply line
Coupling nut
Hot-water shutoff valve
Basin wrench
Cold-water shutoff valve

### Installing a sink faucet

Before you start, have an adjustable wrench on hand. If your new faucet doesn't come with a rubber gasket, you'll also need a supply of plumber's putty.

If you're installing a new faucet on an old sink, make sure the area around the faucet is free of dirt and mineral buildup.

The basic steps in installing a sink faucet are outlined below, but since procedures vary with the type of faucet, you should also look carefully at the manufacturer's instructions.

**Mounting the faucet.** If your new faucet doesn't have a rubber gasket on the bottom, apply a bead of plumber's putty around the underside of the outside edge.

The faucet may have either inlet shanks or inlet tubes and threaded mounting studs. Insert the inlet shanks or tubes down through the holes in the mounting surface; press the faucet onto the surface. For a faucet with inlet shanks, screw the washers and locknuts onto the shanks by hand (see illustration at left); tighten with a wrench. If your faucet has tubes, assemble and tighten the washers and nuts on the mounting studs (see drawing below).

**Connecting the plumbing.** Two types of flexible supply lines are available: chrome-plated corrugated metal tubing and plastic tubing. Because it's a little better looking, metal tubing is usually used when the supply lines are visible. Gaskets and coupling nuts are sold separately, so be sure they fit the faucet and the shutoff valves. Plastic tubing is sold with gaskets and coupling nuts already assembled.

Before connecting the supply lines, apply pipe joint compound to the threads on the inlet shanks and shutoff valves, or to the threads on the fittings at the ends of the tubing.

### INSTALLING A SINGLE-LEVER FAUCET

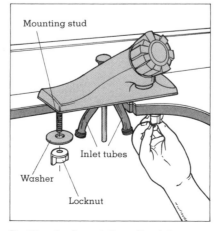

Mounting stud
Inlet tubes
Washer
Locknut

**Position the faucet,** threading inlet tubes through the sink hole; then tighten the locknuts on mounting studs.

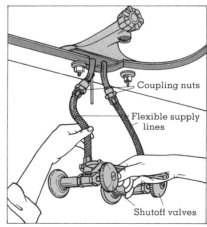

Coupling nuts
Flexible supply lines
Shutoff valves

**Extend flexible tubing** from inlet tubes as required; attach it to shutoff valves with an adjustable wrench.

Then connect the supply lines to the inlet shanks or tubes (see illustration on facing page). Tighten the coupling nuts with a wrench. Gently bend the supply lines to meet the shutoff valves, and secure them to the valves with coupling nuts. Tighten the nuts with an adjustable wrench, then turn on the water and check for leaks.

If you're installing a new pop-up drain assembly, follow the manufacturer's instructions. Connect the pop-up rod to the new pivot rod, using the fastenings supplied with the new drain assembly.

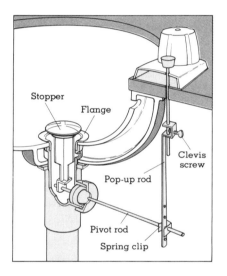

## BATHTUB & SHOWER FAUCETS

Faucets for bathtubs and showers are either compression models (usually with separate hot and cold water controls) or washerless models (with a single lever or knob to control the flow and mix of hot and cold water). In both types (see illustration above right), the faucet body is mounted directly on the water supply pipes inside the wall.

You can either renovate a bathtub or shower faucet, or completely replace it. If the faucet body is in good condition, you may simply want to replace some of the faucet parts. If the faucet body is in poor condition, or if you want to change the type of

**TWO TYPES OF BATHTUB AND SHOWER FAUCETS**

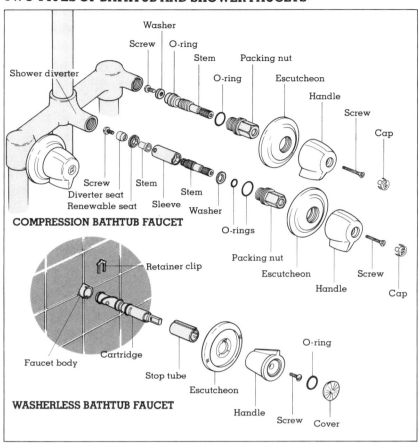

COMPRESSION BATHTUB FAUCET

WASHERLESS BATHTUB FAUCET

faucet you have, you may have to replace the entire assembly. You'll also need to replace the complete faucet if you want to add a shower head above an existing bathtub (see "Adding a shower faucet," page 94). The following sections tell you how to renovate or replace a faucet.

### Renovating a bathtub or shower faucet

To renovate a faucet, you can replace faucet parts—stems, handles, and trim (such as escutcheons)—and the tub spout or shower head. In a tub, you might also replace the diverter—the mechanism that redirects water to the shower pipe. To find the correct replacement parts, it's a good idea to disassemble the old faucet first, then take the parts with you to the store when you shop for new ones.

Before you start work, turn off the water at the bathtub or shower shutoff valves or at the main shutoff valve. (Bathtub or shower shutoff valves may be accessible through a panel in an adjoining room, hall, or closet.)

The drawings on this page show you how typical compression and washerless faucets are put together, but the assembly may vary with individual models. As you disassemble your faucet, take notes and make a sketch of the parts and the sequence of assembly so you'll be able to put the faucet back together. First remove faucet handles, trim, and stem parts; then remove the diverter (if necessary). Finally, remove the tub spout or shower head with a tape-wrapped pipe wrench.

When you're ready to assemble the new fittings, simply reverse the procedure.

*(Continued on next page)*

# ■Faucets

### REMOVING A BATHTUB FAUCET

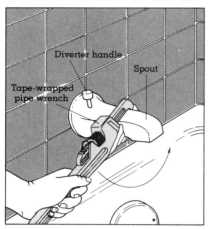

**Remove spout** from wall stubout by turning counterclockwise with a tape-wrapped pipe wrench.

**Remove faucet body** from supply pipes by unscrewing or unsoldering the connections.

## Replacing a bathtub or shower faucet

Replacing a complete bathtub or shower faucet involves cutting away the wall covering and removing the faucet body from the supply pipes with wrenches or a small propane torch. You'll need to take the old faucet body with you when you buy a new one, to be sure of getting the correct size. If you've never done any pipefitting, you may want to get professional help to install the new faucet body.

**Getting to the faucet body.** First remove the faucet handles and trim, and the shower head or tub spout and diverter. To work on the faucet body and the pipes behind the wall, open the access door or panel if one is available. If not, cut a hole in the bathroom wall large enough to allow you to work on the faucet body and pipes comfortably (see illustration at right). Then turn off the water at the bathtub shutoff valves or main shutoff valve.

**Removing the faucet body.** The illustration above shows how a bathtub or shower faucet body is mounted onto the water supply pipes. It may be attached with either threaded or soldered connections. If you find threaded connections, un-

screw them. Use one wrench on the supply pipe to hold it steady, and one wrench on the coupling, turning it counterclockwise. If you find soldered copper connections, unsolder them, using a small propane torch.

**Installing the faucet body.** If your tub or shower is not equipped with individual shutoff valves, you may want to add them now (or consult a professional plumber for help). To install a faucet body on threaded pipe fittings, apply pipe joint compound to the male threads of the pipes and screw the connecting coupling nuts down tight.

For copper pipe, solder couplings to the pipes and screw them onto the faucet body. If the faucet body must be soldered directly to the pipe, first remove the valve and diverter stems.

After the pipes are connected to the faucet body, turn the water on and check for leaks. To make certain the pipes can't vibrate when the water is turned on and off, anchor them and the faucet body firmly to the wall studs or support with pipe straps before patching and recovering the wall.

Carefully measure and mark the positions of the new faucet, spout, and shower head stubouts on the replacement wall covering. Then

prepare and replace the wall covering, and attach the new fittings.

## Adding a shower faucet

To add a shower head above your old bathtub, you'll have to replace the old faucet assembly with one equipped with a shower outlet and diverter valve. In addition, you'll have to install a shower pipe in the wall, as shown below.

If your tub surround is tiled, the tile will have to be removed so you can add the shower pipe. Cut your access hole large enough to install the shower pipe. From the shower outlet on the faucet body, run a ½-inch pipe up the wall to the desired height (see illustration, page 75) and top it with an elbow. Nail a 2 by 4 wood support behind the elbow and anchor the pipe to it with a pipe strap.

To avoid scratching the shower arm while you're repairing the wall covering, thread a 6-inch galvanized nipple into the elbow in place of the shower arm.

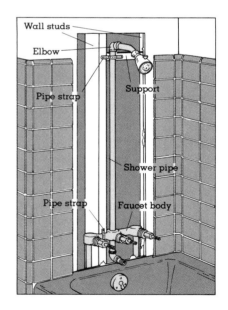

Finally, clean the pipe threads and install the shower arm and shower head, using pipe joint compound on the male threads of the fittings. Repair or replace wall coverings as required (see pages 98–105).

# Toilets & bidets

Removing or installing a toilet or bidet is not very complicated, especially when the plumbing is already in place. During major remodeling involving the floor or walls, remember that toilets and bidets are the first fixtures to remove and the last to install.

For product information on various models, see page 60.

## TOILETS

Conventional two-piece toilets have a floor-mounted bowl with a tank mounted on the bowl. Older types with floor-mounted bowls may have the tank mounted on the wall. One-piece toilets, with the bowl and tank mounted on the floor as a single unit, are becoming increasingly popular with homeowners. (One-piece wall-hung models that connect directly to the stack in the wall are also available.) This section deals primarily with conventional floor-mounted toilets.

Before you begin work, be sure to check any code requirements for a new or replacement toilet.

### Removing a toilet

The procedure for removing a toilet varies with the type of fixture. For a two-piece toilet, you remove the tank first, then the bowl. (For a one-piece toilet, you remove the tank and bowl at the same time.)

**Disconnect the water supply.** Before you begin work, turn off the water at the fixture shutoff valve or main shutoff valve. Flush the toilet twice to empty the bowl and tank; then sponge out any remaining water. To remove the toilet seat and lid, unfasten the nuts on the two bolts projecting down through the bowl's back edge. Unfasten the coupling nut on the water supply line (see illustration below) underneath the tank. If the line is kinked or corroded, replace it when you install the new toilet.

**Remove the tank.** If you're removing a bowl-mounted toilet tank, detach the empty tank from the bowl as follows: Locate the mounting bolts inside the tank at the bottom. Hold them stationary with a screwdriver while you use a wrench to unfasten the nuts underneath the tank (see illustration below). You'll find it easier to remove the nuts if a helper holds the screwdriver. Then lift up the tank and remove it.

In a wall-mounted tank, a pipe usually connects the tank and bowl. Loosen the couplings on the pipe and remove it. Then reach inside the tank with a wrench and unscrew the nuts on the hanger bolts—these attach the tank to the hanger bracket on the wall. Now you can remove the tank.

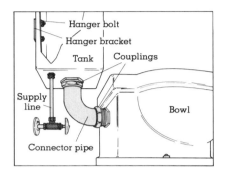

**Remove the bowl.** The following instructions apply to most floor-mounted toilet bowls. At the base of the bowl near the floor, pry off the caps covering the hold-down floor bolts. Unscrew the nuts from the bolts. If the nuts have rusted on, soak them with penetrating oil or cut the bolts off with a hacksaw.

Gently rock the bowl from side to side, breaking the seal between the bowl and the floor. Lift the bowl straight up, keeping it level so any remaining water doesn't spill from its trap (see illustration below).

Stuff a rag into the open drainpipe to prevent sewer gas from escaping and to keep debris from falling into the opening.

*(Continued on next page)*

## REMOVING A FLOOR-MOUNTED TOILET

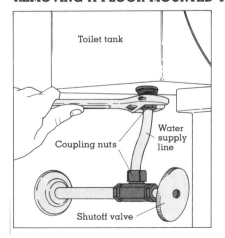

**Loosen the coupling nut** on the water supply line at the bottom of the tank, using a wrench.

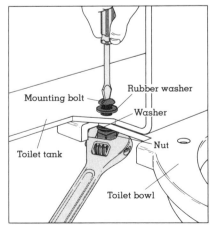

**Detach the tank** from the bowl by loosening mounting bolts with a screwdriver and a wrench.

**Lift the bowl** straight up off the floor flange, keeping it level to avoid spilling any remaining water.

# ■ Toilets & bidets

## Installing a toilet

The amount of work needed to install a new toilet depends on whether it will be in a new location. Hooking up a toilet in a new location is a challenging project because you must extend supply, drain, and vent pipes (see pages 72–75). You may want to have a professional run the piping to the desired spot and then complete the installation yourself.

Replacing an old fixture with a new one at the same location is a one-afternoon project that you can do yourself. The only crucial dimension you need to check on a new toilet is its roughing-in size—the distance from the wall to the center of the drainpipe (most are 12 inches).

You can usually determine roughing-in size before removing the old bowl—just measure from the wall to one of the two hold-down bolts that secure the bowl to the floor. (If the bowl has four hold-down bolts, measure to one of the rear bolts.) Your new toilet's roughing-in size can be shorter than that of the fixture you're replacing, but if it's longer, the new toilet won't fit.

Once you've determined that the fixture will fit, you're ready to install it. The following general instructions apply to two-piece floor-mounted toilets. The key steps are illustrated at right. (For a one-piece, floor-mounted toilet, install the bowl as described below, then connect the water supply.)

**Prepare the floor flange.** This fitting connects the bowl to the floor and drainpipe.

Remove the rags and, with a putty knife, scrape off the wax bowl ring that formed the seal between the bowl and the flange. Thoroughly scrape the flange so that the new ring will form a leakproof seal.

If the old flange is cracked or broken, or if its surface is rough, replace it with a new flange, matched to the existing drainpipe material. (Use a plastic flange with plastic pipe, cast iron with a cast iron pipe.) Remove the old hold-down bolts from the floor flange, then insert the new bolts through the

flange. If necessary, hold them upright with plumber's putty. Align the bolts with the center of the drainpipe.

**Install the bowl ring.** Turn the new bowl upside down on a cushioned surface. Place the new bowl ring over the toilet horn (outlet) on the bottom of the bowl, and apply plumber's putty around the bowl's bottom edge.

**Place the bowl.** Check that all packing material has been removed from the new bowl, and all rags from the drainpipe. Then gently lower the

bowl into place over the flange, using the bolts as guides. To form the seal, press down firmly while twisting slightly.

Check the bowl with a level—from side to side and from front to back; use copper or brass washers to shim underneath the bowl where necessary. Be careful not to break the seal. Hand tighten the washers and nuts onto the hold-down bolts; you'll tighten them permanently after the tank is in place.

**Attach the tank.** For a bowl-mounted tank, fit the rubber gasket

## INSTALLING A FLOOR-MOUNTED TOILET

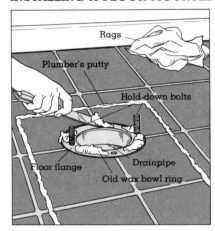

Thoroughly scrape the old bowl ring from the floor flange, using a putty knife or similar tool.

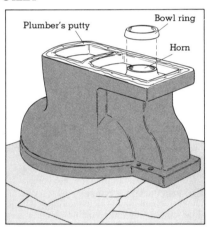

Position the new bowl ring over the toilet horn on the bottom of the bowl as it rests on a cushioned surface.

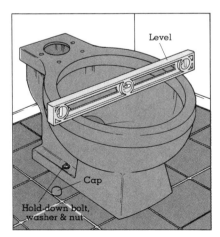

Level the bowl once it's in place, using small copper or brass washers to shim underneath, if necessary.

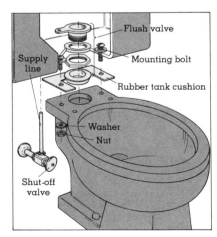

Attach the tank to the bowl using mounting bolts, with rubber gasket and tank cushion in place.

over the end of the flush valve that projects through the bottom of the tank. Place the rubber tank cushion on the rear of the bowl. After positioning the tank on the bowl, insert the mounting bolts through their holes in the bottom of the tank so they pass through the tank cushion and the back of the bowl. Then tighten the nuts and washers onto the bolts. (Secure wall-mounted tanks to hanger brackets with bolts through the back of the tank. Assemble the large pipe between bowl and tank and tighten the couplings.)

Now you can attach the bowl to the floor permanently. Use a wrench to tighten the hold-down nuts at the base of the bowl, but don't overtighten them or you'll crack the bowl. Check to see that the bowl is still level and doesn't rock. Fill the caps with plumber's putty and place them over the nuts. Seal the joint between the base of the bowl and the floor with a bead of caulking compound.

Attach the toilet seat by inserting mounting bolts through the holes in the back of the bowl; then assemble the washers and nuts onto the bolts and tighten.

**Connect the plumbing.** Connect the water supply line to the underside of the tank. If your old plumbing had no fixture shutoff valve, install one now (consult a professional plumber for help). Finally, turn on the water and check for leaks.

## BIDETS

A bidet—a one-piece fixture—is usually installed next to the toilet. Unlike a toilet, a bidet has a sink-type drain and trap and is plumbed for hot and cold water. (For product information, see page 60.)

### Removing a bidet

A bidet is usually not difficult to remove. You just disconnect two water supply lines, a drainpipe, and the hold-down bolts.

**Disconnect the plumbing.** Before doing any work, turn off the

water at the fixture shutoff valves or main shutoff valve. Open all faucets; then unfasten the coupling nuts on the hot and cold water supply lines, so that all remaining water will be completely drained. These lines are either freestanding or attached to the wall behind the bidet. (Some bidets may be plumbed with mixing valves in the wall and a single water supply line running to the fixture.)

Behind and under the back of the bidet, you'll find the drainpipe connection and usually a pop-up drain assembly. First, loosen the clevis screw (see illustration on page 93) and disconnect this assembly. Then loosen the slip nuts on the trap and remove it.

**Remove the bidet.** Pry the caps off the flange at the base of the bidet and remove the nuts underneath them. If the nuts are rusted, soak them with penetrating oil or cut the bolts with a hacksaw.

Lift the bidet straight up off the hold-down bolts that secure it to the floor. You may need to rock the fixture gently first to break the caulk seal (if there is one) around the base.

Stuff a rag into the drainpipe to prevent debris from falling into the opening.

### Installing a bidet

A bidet must be mounted to the floor with hold-down bolts. If you're hooking up a new bidet in an existing location and want to use the existing floor bolts, the distance between bolt holes must be the same as for the original fixture. Also make sure the fittings on the new model are compatible with the existing water supply and drain lines.

If you're installing a bidet in a new location, you'll need to extend supply pipes and drainpipes (see pages 72–75). Unless you're experienced in home plumbing, you'll probably want to hire a professional for this part of the job.

**Position the bidet.** Remove all packing material from the bidet and

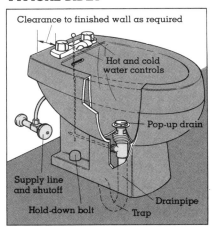

**TYPICAL BIDET**

Clearance to finished wall as required

Hot and cold water controls

Pop-up drain

Supply line and shutoff

Hold-down bolt

Drainpipe

Trap

place the fixture so that its drain opening is directly over the drainpipe. If it's a new installation rather than a replacement, mark the locations for the hold-down bolts on the floor, using the holes in the bidet's flange as guides; then remove the bidet, drill holes sized for the bolts, and screw the bolts through the floor. Turn the bidet upside down onto a cushioned surface and apply plumber's putty around the bottom edge.

Remove the rag from the drainpipe and set the bidet back in position, using the bolts as guides.

Level the bidet, from side to side and from front to back, using copper or brass washers to shim beneath the bottom edge, if necessary. If you do shim, you may need to reseal the fixture to the floor. Hand tighten washers and nuts onto the hold-down bolts; you'll tighten them further after the plumbing connections are made. Connect the pop-up drain assembly, if there is one.

**Connect the plumbing.** Connect the drain and the two water supply lines. Once all connections are made, use a wrench to tighten the nuts on these lines, as well as the nuts on the hold-down bolts. (Don't overtighten the hold-down bolts or you'll crack the fixture.) Fill the caps with plumber's putty and place them over the nuts on the bidet flange. Turn on the water and check for leaks.

# Walls & ceilings

A new moisture-resistant wall or ceiling can improve the bathroom's appearance and make the room easier to maintain at the same time.

This section will show you how to remove and apply the most popular wall treatments in today's bathrooms—gypsum wallboard, wallpaper, and ceramic tile. (For information on painting, see the special feature on page 101.)

## GYPSUM WALLBOARD

This versatile wall covering has a gypsum core faced with thick paper. You can use it as finish material, putting paint or wallpaper over it, or you can use it as a backing for other materials, such as tile, wood, or panels of plastic-coated hardboard.

A special water-resistant grade is available for use around tubs, showers, and other damp areas. This wallboard is usually identified by a blue or green paper cover. It's best not to use it where you plan to paint or wallpaper, though—the compound you must use to finish joints between panels of water-resistant wallboard is nearly impossible to sand, so every imperfection will show through.

Panels are generally 4 feet wide and 8 feet long. (Lengths over 8 feet can be specially ordered.) Common thicknesses are ⅜ inch for wallboard used as a backing, ½ inch for wallboard used as finish wall covering.

## INSTALLING WALLBOARD ON A WALL

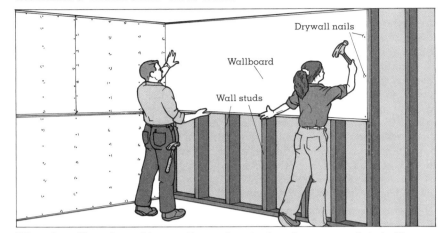

**Lift each wallboard panel** into position and center the edges over wall studs. Then nail the panel to the studs, dimpling the wallboard surface slightly with the hammer. Stagger panels in adjacent rows so that ends don't line up.

### Removing gypsum wallboard

If your bathroom's existing wallboard has only minor cracks or holes, you can probably repair it by filling in the cracks with ready-mixed spackling compound, then sanding smooth. But if it's wet, mildewed, or badly damaged, you'll have to remove it before installing other wall covering.

Use a broad-bladed prybar and a claw hammer to remove wallboard. Wear a dust mask to avoid inhaling gypsum dust, and cover all fixtures and the floor with drop cloths. Finally, be sure to turn off electrical power to the bathroom by flipping a circuit breaker or removing a fuse, so you won't risk hitting a live wire with the prybar.

Your wallboard may be nailed at intervals along the wall studs, or nailed only around the outside edges and sealed to the studs with adhesive. In either case, the removal procedure is the same.

Break through a taped seam between panels with the prybar. Then pry up the panel, using the stud for leverage, until you loosen a large piece. With both hands, pull the piece of wallboard off the studs. (Some of the nails will probably come off with it.) If the wallboard is attached with adhesive, you can leave the backing paper on the studs.

Once you've completely stripped the wallboard away from the studs, work through the area a second time and pull out any remaining nails.

## CUTTING GYPSUM WALLBOARD

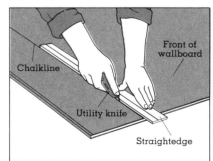

**Cut** wallboard along pencil or chalk line marked on front face, using utility knife guided by straightedge.

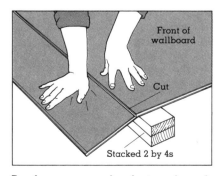

**Break** gypsum core by placing edges of stacked 2 by 4s under cut and pressing down on panel.

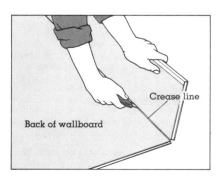

**Complete** cut by turning panel over, bending wallboard back, and cutting through back paper with utility knife.

## INSTALLING WALLBOARD ON A CEILING

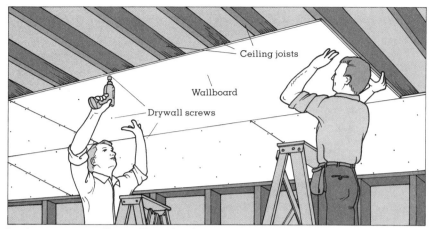

Ceiling joists

Wallboard

Drywall screws

**It takes two to install a wallboard ceiling.** Prop each panel in place with your heads; screw or nail first in the center and then where it will take the weight off your heads.

### Installing gypsum wallboard

Installing gypsum wallboard is a three-step procedure. You measure and cut panels to size, hang them, and finish the seams and corners with wallboard compound and tape. Handle bulky panels carefully as you work; take care not to bend or break the corners or tear the paper covers.

**Cut the wallboard.** Though you'll use some full-size panels, you'll also need to cut pieces to fit around obstacles such as doors, windows, fixtures, and cabinets.

To make a straight, simple cut, first mark a line on the front of the panel with a pencil and straight-edge, or snap a chalkline. Cut through the front paper with a utility knife; use a straightedge to guide the knife. Break the gypsum core by bending the board toward the back, as shown in the drawing on page 98. Finally, cut the paper on the back along the bend. Smooth the cut edge with a perforated rasp.

To fit wallboard around doors, windows, and other openings, measure and mark carefully. Measure from vertical edges of the opening to the edge of the nearest panel or a corner; measure from horizontal edges to the floor. Transfer the measurements to the wallboard and

make the cutout with a keyhole saw. For mid-panel cutouts, drill a pilot hole, then use a keyhole saw to make the cutout.

**Basic wall application.** Wall panels may be positioned either vertically or horizontally—that is, with the long edges either parallel or perpendicular to wall studs. Most professionals prefer the latter method because it helps bridge irregularities between studs and results in a stronger wall. But if your wall is higher than 8 feet, you may not want to use this method, since the extra height requires more cutting and creates too many joints.

Before installing wall panels, mark the stud locations on the floor and ceiling.

Starting at a corner, place the first panel tight against the ceiling and secure it with nails, drywall screws, or construction adhesive supplemented by nails. Drive in nails with a hammer, dimpling the wallboard surface without puncturing the paper. Fastener spacings are subject to local codes, but typical nail spacing is every 8 inches along panel ends and edges and along intermediate supports (called "in the field").

Apply additional panels in the same manner. If you're applying wallboard horizontally, stagger the end

joints in the bottom row so they don't line up with the joints in the top row.

**Basic ceiling application.** Methods for installing a wallboard ceiling are basically the same as those for walls. If you're covering both walls and ceiling, do the ceiling first.

Fasten panels perpendicular to joists with annular ring nails, drywall screws, or a combination of nails and construction adhesive. Screws are quick and strong, but you'll need a power screw gun or drill with adjustable clutch to drive them. Typical fastener spacing is every 7 inches along panel ends and at intermediate joists.

Because you'll need to support the heavy panels while fastening them, installing a wallboard ceiling is a two-person job. First, secure each panel at the center with nails or screws; then place the next few fasteners where they'll take the weight off your heads (see drawing above left).

**Tape the joints and corners.** If your wallboard will be a backing for paneling, you won't need to tape and conceal joints or corners. But if you're painting, wallpapering, or installing tile, you must finish the wallboard carefully. You'll need these basic tools and materials: 6 and 10-inch taping knives, a corner tool, sandpaper, wallboard tape, and taping compound (water-resistant wallboard requires water-resistant compound). See NOTE, page 100, for special instructions on taping water-resistant wallboard.

Finishing is done in stages over a period of days. To tape a joint between panels, first apply a smooth layer of taping compound over the joint with a 6-inch taping knife (see drawing on page 100). Before the compound dries, use the knife to embed wallboard tape into it, and apply another thin coat of compound over the tape, smoothing it gently with the knife.

Tape and finish all joints between panels in the same manner. Then, with smooth, even strokes of

## ■ Walls & ceilings

### TAPING WALLBOARD JOINTS

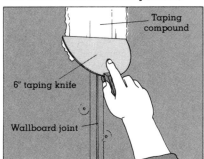

**Apply** a smooth layer of taping compound over wallboard joint, using a 6-inch taping knife.

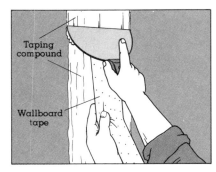

**Embed** wallboard tape into the compound before it dries, and apply another thin layer of compound.

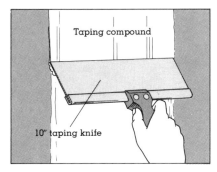

**Apply** a second coat a few inches on each side of joint, feathering compound out to edges.

the 6-inch knife, cover the nail dimples in the field with compound.

Allow the taping compound to dry for at least 24 hours; then sand lightly until the surface is smooth. Wear a face mask and goggles while sanding, and make sure the room is well ventilated.

Now use a 10-inch knife to apply a second coat of compound, extending it a few inches on each side of the taped joint. Feather the compound out toward the edges.

Let the second coat dry, sand it, then apply a final coat. Use the 10-inch knife to smooth out and feather the edges, covering all dimples and joints. Once the compound dries, sand it again to remove even minor imperfections.

NOTE: To finish water-resistant wallboard that will be backing for ceramic tile, first embed the tape in water-resistant taping compound along panel joints; then remove all excess compound with a taping knife. Apply a second thin coat over the wet taping coat and fill any nail dimples. Do not leave excess compound—it can't be sanded dry.

To tape an inside corner, it's easiest to use precreased tape. Apply a smooth layer of compound to the wallboard on either side of the corner. Measure and tear the tape, fold it in half vertically along the prepared crease, and press it into the corner with a taping knife or corner tool. Apply a thin layer of compound over the tape and smooth it out; then finish as you did the other joints.

Nail metal cornerbeads to all exterior corners to protect them. Apply compound to each side of the corner with a 6-inch knife. When it's dry, sand it smooth. With a 10-inch knife, apply a second coat of compound, feathering it. Allow to dry, then sand away imperfections.

**Textured versus smooth finish.** Though many people prefer the smooth look, texture can hide a less-than-perfect taping job—and add some visual interest to an uninterrupted wall. Some joint compounds double as texturing compounds; other effects may require special texturing materials. Ask your dealer for recommendations.

Professionals often apply texturing with a spray gun, but others produce good results by daubing, swirling, or splattering the compound with a sponge, paint roller, or stiff brush—whatever tool produces the desired appearance.

Let the compound set up until slightly stiff; then even it out as required with a wide float or trowel. Allow the finished surface to dry for at least 24 hours before painting.

### Hanging new wallpaper

Next to paint, wallpaper is the most popular covering for bathroom walls. Easier than ever to install, wallpaper is available in a kaleidoscope of colors and patterns.

**Choices for the bathroom.** A wallpaper for the bathroom should be scrubbable, durable, and stain-resistant. Solid vinyl wallpapers, available in a wide variety of colors and textures, fit the bill. Vinyl coatings also give wallpaper a washable surface but aren't notably durable or grease-resistant.

If you're a beginner, you may want to consider prepasted and pretrimmed paper.

To find an adhesive suitable for your material, check the manufacturer's instructions or ask your dealer.

**Preparing the surface.** To prepare for papering, you'll need to remove all light fixtures and faceplates. Thoroughly clean and rinse the surface. Most manufacturers recommend that you completely remove any old wallpaper before hanging a nonporous covering like solid vinyl.

If the existing paper is strippable, it will come off easily when you pull it up at a corner or seam. To remove nonstrippable wallpaper, use either a steamer (available for rent from your dealer) or a spray bottle filled with very hot water. Before steaming, break the surface of the old paper by sanding it with very coarse sandpaper or by pulling a sawblade sideways across the wall.

Within a few minutes of steaming (wait longer if it's a nonporous material), you can begin to remove the old paper. Using a broad knife, work down from the top of the wall, scraping off the old wallpaper.

If yours is a new gypsum wallboard surface, tape all joints between panels before papering. When

# PAINTING: TIPS FOR A PROFESSIONAL FINISH

A fresh coat of paint is the fastest way to brighten up your bathroom. Here are some guidelines to help you do a professional-looking job.

## Selecting tools & materials

One key to a good paint job is to choose the right materials.

**Paint.** Your basic choices in paint are water-base, or latex, paint and oil-base, or alkyd, paint. Latex is easy to work with, and best of all, you can clean up wet paint with soap and water. Alkyd paint provides high gloss and will hang on a little harder than latex; however, alkyds are harder to apply and require cleanup with mineral spirits.

In general, high resin content is the mark of durable, abrasion-resistant, flexible paint—the kind you need in a bathroom. Usually, the higher the resin content, the higher the gloss; so look for products labeled gloss or semigloss if you want a tough, washable finish.

An excellent choice for bathroom cabinets and woodwork is quick-drying alkyd enamel. It has a brilliant, tilelike finish that's extremely durable.

**Tools.** Natural bristle brushes are traditionally used to apply oil-base alkyd enamel paints; synthetic bristles are best for latex products. For window sashes and trim, choose a 1½ or 2-inch angled sash brush. A 2 or 3-inch brush or a paint pad is best for woodwork, doors, and cabinets.

## Preparing the surface

To prevent cracking and peeling after the new paint dries, you must begin with surfaces that are smooth and clean.

It's possible to paint over wallpaper that's smooth and attached firmly to the wall. Apply a sealing primer such as pigmented shellac or a flat oil-base enamel undercoat. Let the sealer dry completely before you paint. It's often safer, though, to remove the wallpaper, especially if it's tearing and flaking.

**Repairing the finish.** For an old painted finish, sanding is sufficient if the surface is flaking lightly. Wash dirty areas on wood surfaces before sanding.

Roughen glossy paint surfaces with sandpaper so the new paint will adhere. (Rough, bare wood also needs sanding, as do patched areas.)

When a wood finish is in such bad condition that painting over it is impossible, you'll have to strip it. You can use an electric paint softener or heat gun, or a commercial liquid paint remover. With either method, you take off the softened paint with a broad knife or scraper, then sand the surface lightly until it's clean and smooth.

Once you've prepared the surface, carefully inspect it for small holes and cracks.

To repair small holes in wallboard, use spackling compound. For details on repairing other surfaces, consult a wall covering specialist.

Finally, dust everything in the bathroom, then vacuum the floor. With an abrasive cleaner, sponge the areas you plan to paint, then rinse. Allow about 24 hours for all washed areas to dry completely.

**Prime the surface.** Before doing any finish painting, be sure to prime the surface. Use the primer recommended by the paint manufacturer for the type of surface you'll be painting.

## Applying the paint

To avoid painting yourself into a corner, you'll want to follow the working sequence outlined below.

**Ceiling.** If you're painting both ceiling and walls, begin with the ceiling. Paint the entire surface in one session. It's best to paint in 2 by 3-foot rectangles, starting in a corner and working across the shortest dimension of the ceiling.

On the first section, use a brush or special corner pad to paint a narrow strip next to the wall line and around any fixtures. Then finish the section with a roller, overlapping any brush marks. Work your way back and forth across the ceiling, painting one section at a time. Then go on to the walls.

**Walls.** Mentally divide a wall into 3-foot-square sections, starting from a corner at the ceiling line and working down the wall. As with ceilings, paint the edges of each section first with a brush or corner roller. Paint along the ceiling line and corners, and around fixtures and edges of doors or windows. Finish each section with a roller or brush, overlapping any brush marks.

At the bottom of the walls above the floor or baseboard, and along the edges of vanities and medicine cabinets, use a brush and painting guide to get a neat, even edge. Be sure to overlap any remaining brush marks with your roller.

As a final step, return to the ceiling line and again work down in 3-foot sections.

## ■ Walls & ceilings

dry, sand the wall smooth and apply a coat of flat, oil-base primer-sealer.

To apply wallpaper over previously painted surfaces that are in good condition, clean off all the dirt, grease, and oil, and let it dry. If latex paint was used, or if you can't determine the type, apply an oil-base undercoat over the old paint.

**Ready to start?** Plan the best place to hang your first strip. If you're papering all four walls with a patterned paper, the last strip you hang probably won't match the first, so plan to start and finish in the least conspicuous place—usually a corner, door casing, or window casing.

Most house walls are not straight and plumb, so you'll need to establish a plumb line. Figure the width of your first strip of wallpaper minus ½ inch (which will overlap the corner or casing); measure that distance from your starting point, and mark the wall. Using a carpenter's level as a straightedge, draw a line through your mark that's perfectly plumb. Extend the line until it reaches from floor to ceiling.

It's a good idea to measure the wall height before cutting each strip of wallpaper. Allow 2 inches extra at the top and bottom. Be sure also to allow for pattern match.

Using a razor knife, cut the strips. Number them on the back at the top edge so you can apply them in the proper sequence.

With some wallpapers, you'll need to spread adhesive on the backing with a wide, soft paint roller or pasting brush; other papers are prepasted—all you have to do is soak them in water before hanging.

After pasting or soaking, strips should be "booked" (see below).

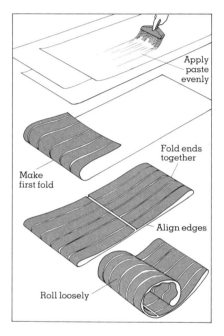

Apply paste evenly

Make first fold

Fold ends together

Align edges

Roll loosely

Trim the edges of the wallpaper at this stage, if necessary.

**Hanging the wallpaper.** First, position a stepladder next to the plumb line you've marked. Open the top fold of the first booked strip, raising it so that it overlaps the ceiling line by 2 inches. Carefully align the strip's edge with the plumb line.

Using a smoothing brush, press the strip against the wall. Smooth out all wrinkles and air bubbles. Then release the lower portion of the strip and smooth it into place.

Carefully roll the edges flat, if necessary, with a seam roller. To trim along the ceiling and baseboard, use a broad knife and a very sharp razor knife. With a sponge dipped in lukewarm water, remove any excess adhesive before it dries.

Unfold your second strip on the wall in the same way you did the first. Gently butt the second strip against the first, aligning the pattern as you move down the wall. Continue around the room.

**Dealing with corners.** Because few rooms have perfectly straight corners, you'll have to measure from the edge of the preceding strip to the corner; do this at three heights. Cut a strip ½ inch wider than the widest measurement. Butting the strip to the

### HANGING THE FIRST STRIP

2" overlap

Plumb line

A

½" overlap

B

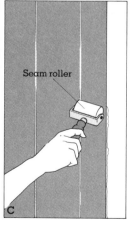

Seam roller

C

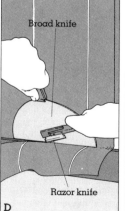

Broad knife

Razor knife

D

Sponge

E

**To hang wallpaper,** first open the top fold of the strip, overlap the ceiling line, and align the strip's edge with the plumb line (A); press the strip against the wall with a smoothing brush (B). Release the lower fold and smooth into place; roll the edges flat with a seam roller (C). Trim the strip along the ceiling and baseboard with a broad knife and a razor knife (D). Remove excess adhesive with a sponge dipped in lukewarm water (E).

preceding strip, brush it firmly into and around the corner. At the top and bottom corners, cut the overlap so the strip will lie flat.

Next, measure the width of the leftover piece of wallpaper. On the adjacent wall, measure the same distance from the corner and make a plumb line at that point.

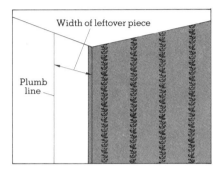

Position one edge of the strip along the plumb line; the other edge will cover the ½-inch overlap. (If you're hanging vinyl wallpaper, you should apply a vinyl-to-vinyl adhesive on top of the overlap.)

**Cutouts.** It's easy to cut around switches and outlets. Remove all faceplates before hanging the wallpaper; then, before making the cutout, shut off the electricity.

Hang the paper as described above. Then use a razor knife to make an X-shaped cut over the opening, extending the cuts to each corner. Trim the excess along the edges of the opening with the razor knife and a broad knife.

## CERAMIC TILE

Few wall coverings have the decorative impact and durability of ceramic tile. It's a natural choice for any wall that might be sprayed or splashed—water, dirt, and soap film clean away in seconds.

On these pages you'll learn how to remove and install ceramic tile. For information on various types of wall tile, see page 63. If your plans call for a ceramic tile floor, install the floor tiles before setting tiles on the wall (see page 108).

### Removing ceramic tile

Removing wall tile set in mortar is a tough job. If possible, replace only those tiles that are damaged. If tiles are clean and smooth and the wall surface is flat, consider installing the new tiles directly over them.

If you must remove old tile, proceed with caution (see "Removing the wall covering" on page 89). You may prefer to have a professional remove tile that is set in mortar.

If your wall tile is set on gypsum wallboard, you can more easily remove it yourself. Wearing goggles and a dust mask, use a cold chisel and soft-headed steel hammer to chip through the tile and backing. Once you've removed small sections, insert a prybar and pry off large sections until the wall studs are exposed.

Next, inspect the exposed wall framing for any water damage, and replace framing members if necessary. Then you can install backing for your new tile or for another wall covering of your choice.

### Installing ceramic tile

Plan and prepare carefully before you install tile. First measure your bathroom and sketch your walls on graph paper. Choose and plan the placement of special trim pieces, such as bullnose, cove, and quarter-round edging tiles, as well as ceramic accessories—soap dishes, paper holders, and toothbrush holders. Your dealer can help you to select trim pieces.

Once you've designed your walls and selected tile, you're ready to begin. Described below are the steps you'll follow to install your tile, from backing to finished wall. (If you're installing pregrouted tile panels, follow the manufacturer's instructions.)

Before you start, remove baseboards and window and door trim, wall-mounted accessories and lights, and, if necessary, the toilet, bidet, and sink.

### Prepare the backing surface.

This is probably the most important step in installing wall tile successfully. Backing must be solid, flat, clean, and dry.

You can use existing gypsum wallboard or even existing wood or tile as backing if it's in good condition. You may need to clean, smooth out, or prime these surfaces before you're ready for new tile; ask your tile dealer for recommendations.

You may also opt for new wallboard backing. But for wet areas, it's safest to install cement backer board, available in 3-foot widths and various lengths. Standard panel thickness for new installations is ½ inch; fasten panels to wall studs with 1½-inch galvanized roofing nails. Fill joints between panels and at edges with thin-set adhesive or mortar. Though it's not strictly necessary, a waterproof membrane behind the backer board helps ensure a watertight wall.

For setting tiles on bathroom walls, choose either thin-set (cement-base) or epoxy adhesive. Thin-set adhesive, when mixed with a latex additive, is adequate for most jobs; epoxy is slightly more difficult to work with and more expensive. The same distinctions apply to cement-base and epoxy grouts. Read the labels and consult your tile dealer to determine which adhesive and grout are best for your situation.

Once your backing is prepared, you're ready to mark working lines.

**Mark working lines.** Accurate horizontal and vertical working lines help you keep tiles properly aligned so that your finished wall will look level and even. The horizontal working line should be near the bottom of the wall, because tiling up a wall is easier than tiling down.

If you're tiling around a tub, establish working lines there first. This way, you can plan for a row of full (uncut) tiles just above the tub, at bathers' eye level. This works out best if the tub is level to within ⅛ inch. Locate the high point of the tub lip with your level, and measure up one tile width plus ⅛ inch. Mark a level line on the wall through this point; then extend it carefully across

## ■ Walls & ceilings

all adjoining walls. This will give you a bottom row of full tiles around the tub. (You can fill in any small gaps below them with caulking later.)

If your tub is not level to within ⅛ inch, locate the horizontal working line from the low point of the tub lip, and follow the above method. You'll have to cut the bottom row of tiles to fit.

Then, on walls adjoining the tub, establish a line close to the floor. Start at the working line you extended from the tub wall and measure down a full number of tiles, including grout joints. Leave a space at least one full tile high above the floor. Mark the horizontal working line for this wall through this point with a straightedge and level (see illustration below).

To establish a line on a wall not adjoining a tub, find the lowest point by setting a level on the floor at various locations against the walls to be tiled. At the lowest point, place a tile against the wall and mark its top edge on the wall. If you're installing a cove base, set a cove tile on the floor and a wall tile above it (allow for grout joint); then mark the top of the wall tile. Using a level and straightedge, draw a horizontal line through the mark across the wall. Extend this line onto other walls to be tiled.

After marking your horizontal working lines, nail battens (1 by 2-

### PATTERNS FOR SETTING TILE

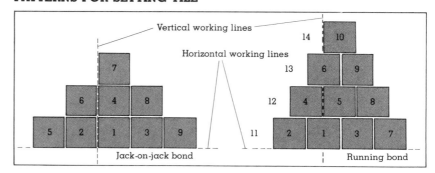

To establish a vertical working line, locate the midpoint of a wall and mark it on the horizontal working line. Starting at this point, set up a row of loose tiles on the batten to see how they'll fit at the ends of the wall.

If you'll end up with less than half a tile on both ends, move your mark one-half a tile to the right or left to avoid ending the rows with narrow pieces. Then extend the vertical working line through your mark and up the wall with a straightedge and level (see illustration below).

If you don't plan to tile to the ceiling line, mark the point where the highest tile will be set. Using a level, draw a horizontal line through this point across the wall.

inch wood strips) all along the walls with their top edges on the lines. These will be your horizontal guides.

Finally, be sure to mark locations of ceramic towel bars, soap dishes, and other accessories.

**Set the tile.** First, prepare the tile adhesive according to the manufacturer's directions. (Be sure to keep your working area well ventilated.)

To determine how large an area to cover at one time, consult the adhesive container label for the open time—the length of time you have to work with the adhesive after spreading. Comb the adhesive with a notched trowel to form ridges.

When you set the tiles, place each one with a slight twist—don't slide it. Keep spacing for grout joints uniform. Some tiles have small ceramic spacing lugs molded onto their edges; if your tiles don't have them, drive 6-penny finishing nails into the wallboard to act as temporary spacing guides (see illustration on facing page).

The way you'll begin setting tiles depends on which bond you use—jack-on-jack (with joints lined up) or running bond (with staggered joints).

For jack-on-jack, set the first tile on the batten so that one side is aligned exactly with the vertical working line. Set additional tiles as shown in the illustration above, forming a pyramid pattern. For running bond, *center* the first tile on the vertical working line, then follow the pyramid pattern (illustrated above), as you set the tile.

With either bond, continue setting tiles upward and toward the ends of the wall in the pattern illustrated. After laying several tiles, set

### WORKING LINES FOR TILE

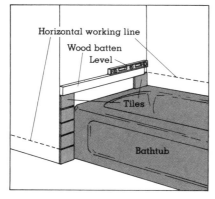

**Extend horizontal working line** around tub to adjoining walls, then measure to floor. Extend lines along adjoining walls.

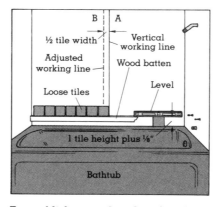

**To establish vertical working line,** locate midpoint of wall (A), then adjust (B) according to size of end tiles.

them into the adhesive by sliding a carpet-wrapped piece of plywood across the tiles as you tap it gently with a hammer.

Cut tiles to fit at the end of each horizontal row and at the top near the ceiling. (Use a rented tile cutter to cut straight pieces; use tile nippers to cut out irregular shapes.) For the top row of a wainscoting or other installation that doesn't reach the ceiling, set bullnose or cap tiles.

When you come to a wall where there are electrical outlets or switches, turn off the power to them. Remove the cover plates, if installed, and pull the outlets and switches from their boxes, but don't disconnect them. Cut and fit tiles around the boxes, then remount the outlets and switches.

On inside corners, butt tiles together. On outside corners, set one column of bullnose tiles to cover the unfinished edges of the tiles on each adjoining wall.

## INSTALLING WALL TILE

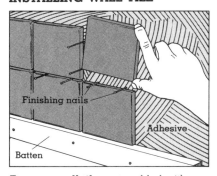

**To space wall tiles** not molded with spacing lugs, place 6-penny finishing nails between tiles.

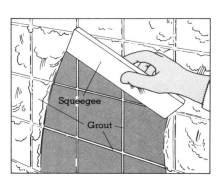

**Spread grout on tile,** forcing it into joints with a float or squeegee until they're full. Remove excess.

Around windows, finish off the sides and sill with bullnose tiles cut to fit.

Install ceramic accessories such as soap dishes in spaces you left open when tiling. Tape the accessories in place while the adhesive sets.

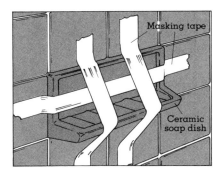

Now check your work. If anything is out of alignment, wiggle it into position before the adhesive sets. Clean adhesive from the face of

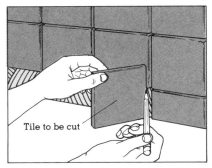

**To set bottom row of tiles,** remove batten on working line, mark tile and cut. Set in adhesive as for other tiles.

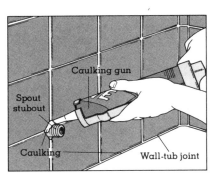

**Use bathtub caulk** to seal all openings between fixtures or pipes and tile.

tiles and accessories, and from joint spaces.

When the adhesive has set, carefully remove the battens. Twist nail spacers as you pull them out from the wall.

Spread adhesive at the bottom of the wall where the battens were, and set the remaining tiles, cutting them as needed.

**Grout the tile.** Before grouting, allow the adhesive to set properly—usually, you must allow 16 hours for epoxy-base adhesive and 48 hours for the cement-base type.

Remove any excess adhesive from the tile joints. Then mix the grout recommended for your tile, and spread it on the surface of the tile with a rubber-faced float or a squeegee, forcing it into the tile joints until they're completely filled. Scrape off excess grout from the tile, working diagonally across the surface.

Wipe the tiles with a wet sponge to remove any remaining grout. Rinse and wring out the sponge frequently, wiping until the grout joints are smooth and level with the tile surface. When the tiles are as clean as you can get them, let the grout dry until a haze appears over the surface. Then polish the haze off the tiles with a soft cloth. Finish (tool) the joints with the end of a toothbrush handle.

**Seal tile and grout.** Installations with unglazed tile or with cement-based grouts need to be protected by a grout and tile sealer. Most sealers for bathroom tile have a silicone base.

Follow manufacturer's instructions for applying these sealers. Both tiles and grout should be dry. On new tile, wait at least 2 weeks—this will give the grout a chance to cure completely. Apply a moderate amount of sealer, and wipe off any excess to prevent the tile from discoloring.

Finally, use caulking to seal all openings or gaps between pipes or fixtures and tile. Replace all trim, accessories, and fixtures.

# Flooring

Two requirements for bathroom floors are moisture resistance and durability. Resilient flooring and ceramic tile are ideal choices on both counts. If you're completely remodeling your bathroom, it's a good time to put in ceramic tile, since it's ideally installed with cabinets, doors, and fixtures removed from the room. If you're replacing only the floor, resilient flooring is a good choice; it can be installed around most fixtures and cabinets.

The information in this section assumes that your floor is supported by a standard subfloor, with joists or beams below (see drawing on page 67). If your home is built on a concrete slab and your flooring will be installed over it, you need to make sure that the slab is dry, level, and clean before you begin any work.

## RESILIENT SHEET FLOORING

Resilient sheet flooring is available with smooth or textured surfaces, in plain colors or in patterns. Though a few types are available in widths up to 12 feet, most sheet flooring is only 6 feet wide; seams may be necessary.

**Plan the new floor.** Take exact measurements of the floor and make a scale drawing on graph paper. If your room is very irregular, you may want to make a full-size paper pattern of the floor instead of the scale drawing.

**Prepare the subfloor.** Both old resilient and wood flooring make acceptable bases for new resilient sheets, provided their surfaces are completely smooth and level. Old resilient flooring must be solid, not cushioned, and firmly bonded to the subfloor. Uneven wood floors may need a rough sanding. Both types must be thoroughly cleaned, and any loose pieces must be secured.

If the old floor is cushioned or in poor condition, it should be removed down to the subfloor, if possible. If the old flooring is impossible to remove without damaging the sub-

floor, or if the subfloor is in poor condition, cover the old flooring with ¼-inch underlayment-grade plywood or untempered hardboard. (If there are signs of water damage or insect infestation, consult a professional.)

**Cut the flooring.** The most critical step in laying sheet flooring is making the first rough cuts accurately. You may want your flooring dealer to make these first cuts for you; if so, you'll need to supply a floor plan.

To cut the flooring to size yourself, unroll the material in a large room. Transfer the floor plan directly onto the new flooring, using chalk or a water-soluble felt-tip pen, a carpenter's square, and a straightedge.

If your flooring will have a seam, be sure to allow for overlap or for matching the pattern (if any) on adjoining sheets. If your flooring has simulated grout or mortar joints, plan to cut the seam along the midpoint of the joint.

Using a linoleum or utility knife, cut the flooring so it's roughly 3 inches oversize on all sides (the excess will be trimmed away after the flooring has been put in place).

Cut 3" extra

Actual room size

If a seam is necessary, cut and install the piece of flooring that requires the most intricate fitting first; then cut and install the second sheet.

**Install the flooring.** Following are instructions for laying resilient sheet flooring using adhesive. Some types of sheet flooring can be laid *without* adhesive. In this case, you simply roll out the flooring and shift

it until it's in the proper position, then apply adhesive around the edges or staple the edges in place. If you're considering this easy installation method, check with your flooring dealer to be sure the material you've selected doesn't require adhesive.

If you're installing a single piece of flooring, you can spread adhesive over the entire subfloor at once, or spread adhesive in steps as the flooring is unrolled. Check the adhesive's open time (the time you have to work with the adhesive while it's still tacky); follow the directions of the adhesive manufacturer.

If the entire floor has been covered with adhesive, slowly roll the flooring out across the floor, taking care to set the flooring firmly into the adhesive as you go. If you're working a section at a time, spread adhesive and unroll the flooring as you go.

If you're installing flooring with seams, spread the adhesive on the subfloor as directed by the adhesive manufacturer, but stop 8 or 9 inches from the seam. Then position the first sheet on the floor.

Next, position the second sheet of flooring carefully so that it overlaps the first sheet by at least 2 inches; make sure the design is perfectly aligned. Then roll up the flooring and spread adhesive over the remainder of the floor, stopping 8 or 9 inches from the edge of the first sheet of flooring. Reposition the second sheet of flooring, starting at the seam; again, take care to align the design perfectly. Then roll the flooring out, setting it into the adhesive.

When the flooring is in position, trim away excess flooring at each end of the seam in a half-moon shape so ends butt against the wall.

Using a steel straightedge and a sharp utility knife, make a straight cut (about ½ or ⅝ inch from the edge of the top sheet) down through both sheets. Lift up the flooring on either side of the seam, remove the two overlap strips, and spread adhesive on the subfloor under the seam.

Use the recommended solvent to clean adhesive from around the seam. When the seam is dry and

## TRIMMING RESILIENT SHEETS

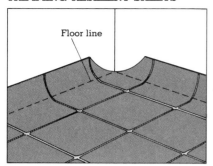

**To trim inside corners,** cut excess flooring away a little at a time until flooring lies flat in corner.

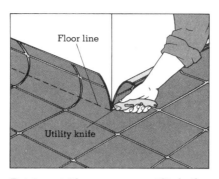

**To trim outside corners,** use utility knife to cut straight down to where wall and floor meet.

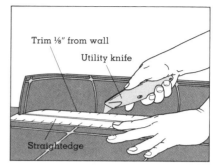

**To trim along walls,** cut flooring with a utility knife and straightedge, leaving a ⅛-inch gap for expansion.

clean, use the recommended seam sealer to fuse the two pieces.

**Trim to fit.** When the flooring has been positioned, you'll need to make a series of relief cuts at all corners so the flooring will lie flat (see above).

At outside corners, start at the top of the excess flooring and cut straight down to the point where the wall and floor meet. At inside corners, cut the excess flooring away a little at a time until it lies flat.

To remove the excess flooring along a wall, press the flooring into a right angle where the floor and wall join, using an 18 to 24-inch-long piece of 2 by 4. Then lay a heavy metal straightedge along the wall and trim the flooring with a utility knife, leaving a gap of about ⅛ inch between the edge of the flooring and the wall to allow the material to expand without buckling.

## RESILIENT TILE FLOORING

Resilient tiles come in two standard sizes, 9-inch and 12-inch square. Other sizes and shapes are available by special order.

To find the amount of tile you need, find the area of the floor, subtracting for any large protrusions. Add 5 percent so you'll have extra tiles for cutting and later repairs. If your design uses more than one color, estimate how many tiles of each kind you'll need by drawing your design with colored pencils.

**Place the tiles.** Laying resilient tiles involves three steps: marking the working lines, spreading the adhesive (unless you're using self-stick tiles), and placing the tiles. These steps are similar to those for ceramic tile (for details, see page 108). But unlike ceramic units, resilient tiles are laid tightly against each other, and, because they're made with machine precision, they must be laid out in perfectly straight lines.

Once a tile is in position, press it firmly in place. Lay half a dozen or so, setting them by going over them with a rolling pin. If you're using self-stick tiles, take extra care to position them exactly before you press them into place (they're hard to remove once they're fixed to the floor). Also note the arrows on the back of self-stick tiles—lay the tiles with the arrows going the same way.

**Cut the tile.** To cut tiles, score them along the mark with a utility knife; then snap the tile along the line. For intricate cuts, use heavy scissors. (The tiles will cut more easily if warmed in sunlight or over a furnace vent.)

To mark border and corner tiles for cutting, position a loose tile exactly over one of the tiles in the last row closest to the wall (see below). Place another loose tile on top of the first, butting it against the wall. Using this tile as a guide, mark the tile beneath for cutting.

## TRIMMING RESILIENT TILES

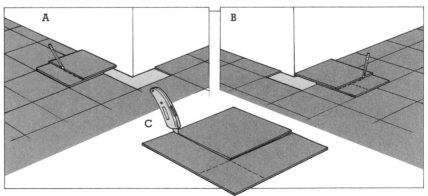

**To lay out a border tile,** first place a loose tile on top of the last full tile nearest the wall; then place a second tile over the first, butting it against the wall, and mark it for cutting (A). This same technique can be used to mark L-shaped tiles for outside corners (B). Score tiles with a utility knife (C).

# ■Flooring

## CERAMIC TILE FLOORING

Installing a new floor of ceramic tile can be a very satisfying do-it-yourself project. New, easy-to-install tiles and improved adhesives and grouts make it possible for a careful, patient do-it-yourselfer to create a floor of professional quality.

Because it's usually possible to use existing ceramic tile as a subfloor (see "Prepare the subfloor," below), this section covers installation only—not removal. It's not easy to remove an old tile floor, particularly if the tiles were laid in mortar. So if removal is necessary, it's best to consult a professional.

Installing a ceramic tile floor is essentially a three-step operation: you lay evenly spaced tiles in a bed of adhesive atop a properly prepared subfloor, fill the joint spaces between tiles with grout, and seal the floor for durability and easy cleaning. In this section you'll find basic instructions for laying tile flooring; if you need more detailed information, turn to a contractor or your tile supplier.

**Prepare the subfloor.** Ceramic tile, masonry, wood, and resilient (except the cushion type) floors can be successfully covered with ceramic tile—provided the old floor is well-bonded, level, clean, and dry.

If the existing flooring is in poor condition, you'll need to repair, cover, or remove it before you can proceed. Fasten loose ceramic, masonry, or resilient flooring with adhesive; nail down loose wood flooring; fill gouges in resilient flooring; and sand wood floors smooth.

If the existing flooring is so badly damaged that it's beyond repair—or if a cushioned resilient flooring has been used—it will need to be removed down to the subfloor, if possible. If the old flooring is impossible to remove without damaging the subfloor underneath, or if the subfloor is in poor condition, you can cover the old flooring with ¼-inch underlayment-grade plywood or untempered hardboard.

Your tile dealer can recommend the best adhesive for your new tile floor (the type of adhesive depends on the type of flooring you'll be covering). Follow your dealer's instructions for preparing the subfloor, and be sure to check the directions on the adhesive container, as well.

**Establish working lines.** The key to laying straight rows of tile is to first establish accurate working lines. Following are instructions for laying out working lines starting from the center of the room. This method makes it easy to keep rows even and is the best method to use if the room is out of square or if you've chosen a tile with a definite pattern or design.

Locate the center point on each of two opposite walls, and snap a chalk line on the floor between the two points. Then find the centers of the other two walls and stretch your chalk line at right angles to the first line; snap this line only after you've used a carpenter's square to determine that the two lines cross at a precise right angle. If they don't, adjust the lines until they do.

Make a dry run before you actually set the tiles in adhesive. Lay one row of tiles along each working line, from the center of the room to each of two adjoining walls. Be sure to allow proper spacing for grout joints. Adjust your working lines as necessary to avoid very narrow border tiles.

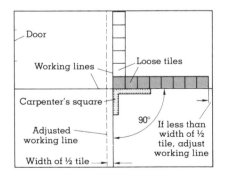

If you're working over a wood subfloor, temporarily nail batten boards along the two working lines that outline the quarter of the room farthest from the door; the battens will provide a rigid guide for the first row of tiles. (If you're working over a masonry subfloor, you'll have to use the chalk lines as your guides.) You'll set tiles using the sequence shown below, completing the floor quarter by quarter. Work on the quarter by the doorway last.

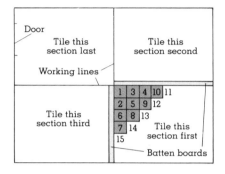

**Set the tiles.** Using a notched trowel, start spreading adhesive. Cover about a square yard at first, or the area you can comfortably tile before the adhesive begins to set.

Using a gentle twisting motion, place the first tile in the corner formed by the two battens (or chalk lines). With the same motion, place a second tile alongside the first. Continue laying tiles, following the sequence illustrated. Use molded plastic spacers to establish the proper width for the grout joints.

As the tiles are laid, set a piece of carpet-wrapped wood over them, and gently tap the wood with a mallet or hammer to "beat in" the tiles. Keep checking with a carpenter's square or straightedge to make sure each row is straight. Wiggle any stray tiles back into position.

To fit border tiles, measure each space carefully, subtract the width of two grout joints, and mark each tile for any necessary cuts.

When you complete the first quarter of the floor, remove the batten boards, then proceed with the next quarter. After all the tiles are placed, remove the spacers and clean the tile surface so it's completely free of adhesive.

Grout and seal the tile according to the instructions for wall tile on page 105.

# Cabinets & countertops

In many homes, the need for bathroom storage has increased as people have collected more and more paraphernalia—bulky electric grooming appliances, children's bath toys, and cleaning supplies. For many families, a medicine cabinet just doesn't provide enough space.

This section will show you how to gain space by installing floor-mounted vanity cabinets, then topping them with countertops of plastic laminate or ceramic tile.

## VANITY CABINETS

You can select a vanity cabinet to complement almost any style of bathroom. The vanity may be fitted with various types of countertops and sinks (see pages 54–56).

No matter what countertop and sink you prefer, the methods for removing and installing a prefabricated vanity cabinet in your bathroom are the same.

If a vanity cabinet higher than standard height is more comfortable, add a frame of suitable height underneath the bottom before installing the cabinet.

### Removing a vanity cabinet

To remove a plumbed vanity, you'll need to disconnect the plumbing and remove the sink and countertop (see pages 82–83).

Pry away any vinyl wall base, floor covering, or molding from the base cabinet's kickspace or sides.

Old vanity cabinets are usually attached to wall studs with screws or nails through nailing strips at the back of each unit. Sometimes they're also fastened to the floor. Screws are easy to remove unless they're old and stripped. To remove nails, you may need to pry the cabinet away from the wall or floor with a prybar. To prevent damage, use a wood scrap between the prybar and the wall or floor. For a vanity with a solid back, you may have to first shut off the water at the main valve and remove the sink shutoff valves to pull the vanity away from the wall.

### Installing a vanity cabinet

Before you begin, remove any baseboard, moldings, or wall base that might interfere. From the floor, measure up 34½ inches—the height of a standard vanity cabinet. Take several measurements and use the highest mark for your reference point. Draw a level line through the mark and across the wall.

If the vanity has a solid back, measure, mark, and cut the holes for the drain and water supply pipes, using a keyhole or saber saw.

For both solid and open-back vanities, locate and mark all wall studs (see page 68) in the wall above where the vanity will be installed. Move the vanity into place.

Level the top of the vanity side-to-side and front-to-back, shimming between the vanity and floor as needed. Both shims and irregularities in the floor can be hidden by baseboard trim.

Some cabinets are designed with "scribing strips" along the sides. Other manufacturers offer decorative panels to "finish" the end of a cabinet run. Both designs include extra material you can shave down to achieve a perfect fit between the cabinet and an irregular wall.

To scribe a cabinet, first position it; then run a length of masking tape down the side to be scribed. Setting the points of a compass with pencil to the widest gap between the scribing strip and the wall, run the compass pivot down the wall next to the strip, as illustrated below. The wall's irregularities will be marked on the tape. Remove the vanity from the wall and use a block plane, file, or power belt sander to trim the scribing strip to the line. Then reinstall the cabinet.

If your cabinet doesn't have scribing strips, you can cover any large irregularities between the wall and cabinet with decorative molding. Scribe the molding as required.

When the cabinet is aligned with your reference marks on the wall, extend the stud location marks down to the hanger strip on the back of the vanity, drill pilot holes through the strip into the wall studs, and secure the vanity to the studs with woodscrews or drywall screws. If the studs aren't accessible, fasten the vanity with wall anchors.

Once the vanity cabinet is secure, install the countertop and sink, then connect the water supply lines, the trap, and the pop-up drain (see pages 83–85).

## INSTALLING A VANITY CABINET

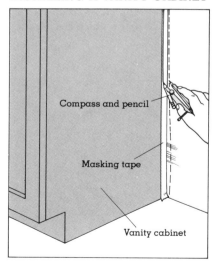

**Scribe and trim** sides of vanity to make a snug fit when wall is out of plumb or is uneven.

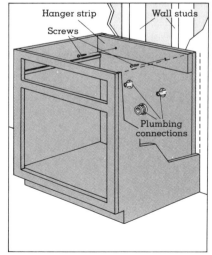

**Secure vanity cabinet** to studs by screwing through hanger strip across the back. Drill pilot holes first.

# ■ Cabinets & countertops

### POST-FORMED LAMINATE COUNTERTOP

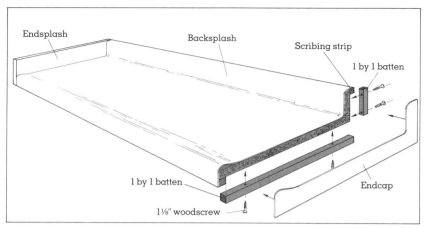

## COUNTERTOPS

Plastic laminate and tile are two popular materials for countertops. Both are durable, water-resistant, and straightforward to install.

### Installing a plastic laminate countertop

Laminate countertops are divided into two types: post-formed and self-rimmed. Post-formed countertops are premolded one-piece tops, from curved backsplash to bullnosed front. The term "self-rimmed" means that you apply the laminate of your choice over a core material.

**Post-formed countertop.** Since post-formed countertops come only

in standard sizes, you'll normally need to buy one slightly larger than you need and cut it to length. To cut the countertop with a handsaw, mark the cut line on the face. Mark the back if you're using a power saw. Use masking tape to protect the cutting line against chipping (you'll probably have to redraw the line, this time on the tape). Smooth the edge of the cut with a file or sandpaper. Plan to cover that end with an endsplash or endcap (a preshaped strip of matching laminate).

Endsplashes are screwed into the edge of the countertop or into "built-down" wood battens attached to the edge, as shown above. Endcaps are glued to an open end with contact cement or, in some cases, pressed into place with a hot iron.

Countertops, like cabinets, rarely fit uniformly against walls. Usually, the back edge of a post-formed countertop comes with a scribing strip that can be trimmed to follow the exact contours of the wall. Follow the instructions for scribing cabinets on page 109.

Fasten the countertop to the cabinets by running screws from below through the cabinet corner gussets or top frame and through any shims or wood blocks. Use woodscrews just long enough to penetrate ½ inch into the countertop core. Run a bead of silicone sealant along all exposed seams between the countertop and walls.

**Self-rimmed countertop.** To build your own laminate countertop, you'll need to choose the laminate (¹⁄₁₆-inch thickness is the standard) and cut the core material to size from ¾-inch plywood or high-density particle board.

Build down the edges of the core with 1 by 3 battens (see drawing below). Then you can laminate the countertop (do sides and front strips first and then the top surface).

Measure each surface to be laminated, adding at least ¼ inch to all dimensions as a margin for error. Mark the cutting line. Score the line with a sharp utility knife; then cut with a fine-toothed saw (face up with a handsaw or table saw, face down with a circular saw or saber saw).

Apply contact cement to both the laminate back and the core surface to be joined, and allow the cement to dry for 20 to 30 minutes. Carefully check alignment before joining the two; once joined, the laminate can't be moved. Press the laminate into place, using a roller or a rolling pin to ensure even contact.

Use a block plane to trim the laminate flush with the core's edges; then dress it with a file. Or trim with an electric router equipped with a laminate-trimming bit.

Backsplashes or endsplashes should be cut from the same core material as the main countertop, then butt-joined to the countertop with sealant and woodscrews.

### SELF-RIMMED LAMINATE COUNTERTOP

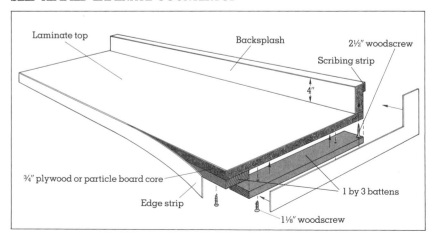

## Installing a ceramic tile countertop

Wall tiles, lighter and thinner than floor tiles, are the normal choice for countertops and backsplashes. Standard sizes range from 3 inches by 3 inches to 4½ inches by 8½ inches, with thicknesses varying from ¼ inch to ⅜ inch. Another choice, mosaic tiles (see page 63), makes your job easier, especially in backsplash areas.

**Prepare the base.** Before laying tile, remove any old countertops; then install ¾-inch exterior plywood cut flush with the cabinet top, screwing it to the cabinet frame from below. For moisture-tight results, add a waterproof membrane, followed by a layer of cement backer board on top.

Surfaces may need to be primed or sealed before tile is applied. To determine the best base and preparation for your job, read the information on the adhesive container or ask your tile supplier.

**Plan the layout.** Before you start laying tile, you must decide how you want to trim the countertop edge and the sink. For ideas, see the drawing below.

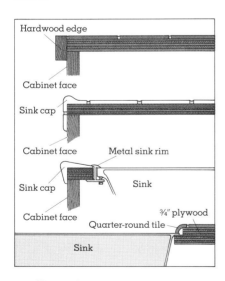

Hardwood edge

Cabinet face

Sink cap

Cabinet face    Metal sink rim

Sink cap    Sink

Cabinet face    ¾" plywood

Quarter-round tile

Sink

If you decide to use wood trim, seal the wood and attach it to the cabinet face with finishing nails. When in place, the wood strip's top edge should be positioned at the

### HOW TO SET COUNTERTOP TILES

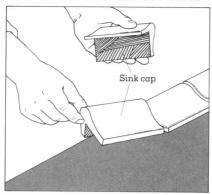

Sink cap

**First, set edge tiles** in place, starting from the center line, after buttering the backs with adhesive.

same height as the finished tile. A recessed sink, commonly used with tile countertops, is also installed at this time (see page 85).

On the front edge of your plywood base, locate and mark the point where the center of the sink or midpoint of a blank countertop will be. Lay the edge tiles out on the countertop, starting from your mark. Some tiles have small ceramic lugs molded onto their edges to keep spacing equal; if your tiles don't, use plastic spacers, available from your tile supplier.

Carefully position the rest of the "field" tiles on the countertop. Observing the layout, make any necessary adjustments to eliminate narrow cuts or difficult fits.

If the countertop will have a backsplash or will turn a corner, be sure to figure the cove or corner tiles into your layout.

Mark reference points of your layout on the plywood base to help you re-create it later; then remove the tile.

**Set the tiles.** Set all trim tiles before spreading adhesive for the field tiles. Thin-set adhesive, mixed with latex additive, is water-resistant and easy to use.

Butter the back of each front-edge tile and press it into place, aligning it with the reference marks. If your edge trim consists of two tile rows, set the vertical piece first.

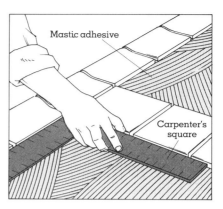

Mastic adhesive

Carpenter's square

**Next, install field tiles.** Use a square to keep the tiles perpendicular to the edge trim.

Next, butter any back cove tiles and set them against the wall. If you've installed a recessed sink, lay the sink trim next. Be sure to caulk between the sink and the base before setting the trim. If you're using quarter-round trim, you can either miter the corners or use special corner pieces available with some patterns.

Spread adhesive over a section of the countertop. Begin laying the field tiles, working from front to back (see illustration, above). Cut tiles to fit as necessary. As you lay the tiles, check the alignment frequently with a carpenter's square.

To set the tiles and level their faces, slide a 1-foot-square scrap of cloth-covered plywood over them and tap the scrap with a hammer.

Unless you're tiling up to an overhead cabinet or window sill, use bullnose tiles for the last row. If a wall contains electrical switches or plug-in outlets, you can cut tiles in two and use tile nippers to nip out a hole.

**Apply the grout.** Remove any spacers and clean the tile surface and grout joints until they're free of adhesive. Allow thin-set adhesive to set for 24 hours before grouting the joints. For details on grouting tools and techniques, see page 105.

After grouting, wait at least 2 weeks for the grout to cure; then apply a recommended sealer.

# Index